SOUL FOOD ODYSSEY

Also by Stephanie L. Tyson

Well, Shut My Mouth! The Sweet Potatoes Restaurant Cookbook

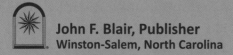
John F. Blair, Publisher
Winston-Salem, North Carolina

Odyssey

Stephanie L. Tyson

JOHN F. BLAIR,
PUBLISHER
1406 Plaza Drive
Winston-Salem, North Carolina 27103
www.blairpub.com

Library of Congress Cataloging-in-Publication Data
Tyson, Stephanie L.
  Soul food odyssey / by Stephanie L. Tyson.
    pages   cm
  Includes index.
   ISBN 978-0-89587-646-1 (alk. paper) — ISBN 978-0-89587-647-8 (ebook)   1.   African American cooking. I. Title.
   TX715.2.A47T97 2015
   641.59'296073—dc23
                              2015010308

10 9 8 7 6 5 4 3 2 1

COVER DESIGN
Debra Long Hampton, Anna Sutton, and Sally Johnson
COVER AND TEXT GRAPHICS
Frames: ©prapass, ©Aleksandrs Bondars, ©akarapong / Shutterstock
Chalkboards: ©Seita / Shutterstock
Artwork: ©T30 Gallery and ©Goldenarts / Shutterstock

PRINTED IN CANADA

*This book is dedicated to my mom, Donzella Tyson,
who continues to feed our souls.*
SEPTEMBER 22, 1933–MARCH 11, 2015

CONTENTS

ACKNOWLEDGMENTS   Ix

INTRODUCTION THE ODYSSEY BEGINS   1

CHAPTER 1 THE SOULFUL PIG—FROM THE ROOTER TO THE TOOTER 9

CHAPTER 2 SOUL MATES—CHICKEN, COW, AND THE FISHES

  IN THE SEA   35

CHAPTER 3 VEGGIE SOUL   67

CHAPTER 4 STONE SOUL SIDES   85

CHAPTER 5 HUMBLE BREAD, FEED MY SOUL   103

CHAPTER 6 THE SOUL-STIRRING POT: SOUPS AND STEWS   121

CHAPTER 7 DESSERTS TO SELL YOUR SOUL FOR   139

CHAPTER 8 SOULFUL CELEBRATIONS—MENUS TO PONDER   163

INDEX   172

Acknowledgments

Vivián is my muse, and I thank her. She is also my taster, and I apologize for the extra pounds she gained from the desserts chapter.

I'd also like to thank my good friends Ruth, Pamela, Tracy, Toni, Ellen, and Robin for aiding in the preparation of recipes and highlighting my "oopses."

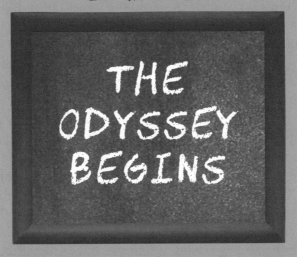

THE ODYSSEY BEGINS

A lot has been said about soul food lately, much of it unflattering. At the very least, most of what is said is one-dimensional.

For many years, my own views mirrored these suggestions that soul food is somehow inferior. When I was young, I was exposed to soul food but didn't think much about it. The Winston-Salem, North Carolina, where I grew up had a self-sustaining "colored" community. We had grocery stores, clothiers that came directly to your door, and funeral homes. We were the only city in the country that had a black-owned city bus company—Safe Bus. We had restaurants such as Ma Chris, the Lincoln Grill, the Alhambra Grill (where my parents met), and Bud's Diner, which served pickled pigs' feet, chitterlings, pinto beans, and, if you were lucky, crackling cornbread.

At one point, there were at least forty-five black-owned cafés in town. My grandmother Ora Porter worked at Bud's Diner. It was open late so customers could get good, sobering food when the drink establishments (liquor houses) turned in for the night. She made pinto beans with broth as thick as pudding and fried chicken so golden and light it put the sun to shame. My grandmother cooked soul food, but that's not what she called it. She just called it "sump'n-ta-eat."

When my brothers and I got a little older, my mom told us she was not cooking on Saturdays. She cooked for us and worked all week, so on Saturdays, if we wanted anything other than peanut butter and jelly, we needed to go to my grandmother's house so my mom could prepare for church and Sunday dinner. My grandmother always had a big pot of something on the stove and fried chicken and fatback in the oven. She actually fried chicken every day, but I rarely saw her eat it. That was true food of the soul.

An old lady who lived up the street from us kept chickens. We saw these chickens in her yard every day when we came home from school. One day, she killed one and gave it to my mom. It freaked my brothers and me out. We refused to eat chicken for a year. We were city kids! We weren't raised eating farm-to-table, but more like A&P-to-table—with cute placemats. To this day, I believe my brothers think that broccoli grows in a frozen box with cheese sauce. But I am evolving.

Right after high school, I left home for college at East Carolina in Greenville, North Carolina—far away enough not to smell the collard greens and neck bones from my grandmother's kitchen but close enough for care packages and frequent visits home. At first, I ate a lot of food that was not so good. I knew how to make only Oodles of Noodles, but I soon discovered a place off campus I could afford that served all-you-can-eat fried chicken and a new taste for me—sweet potato biscuits. With the aid of our backpacks, my clever and hungry classmates and I could pay one price and eat well for a week.

Once I left the South for New York, I left behind my connection to Southern food. I was an aspiring actor, and my goal was to lose that accent. In doing so, I believe I lost my Southern sense and graciousness. Instead, I took on a Northern attitude and edginess.

The interesting thing about New York is that it is full of transplants from everywhere. Certain parts of the city reflect that—Little Italy, Chinatown, the East Village with its Eastern European influence, and Harlem, which was the soul of the Northern South.

The food in Harlem came with the African-Americans during the Great Migration between 1915 and 1970, when millions of blacks left rural parts of the South looking for a better way of life in the big cities. I found in Harlem the food I had grown up with. Places such as Sylvia's Restaurant were going strong, but I was not buying any of it. I had to lose that accent and become a starving actor. I had to fit in with the people whose accents were blank canvases; at least that's what the acting teachers said. I spent years disconnected from food, starving myself sometimes to keep thin and viable. I was not only denying that I was Southern, I was also denying myself highly seasoned soul food. If food didn't come from a deli, diner, or stand, I didn't eat it. I don't think I so much as fried an egg the entire time I lived in New York.

I never realized my connection to food and history was gone until I returned home deflated, defeated, and hungry. New York didn't exactly kick me out, but really, how many people do you need who sound alike and look alike, all vying for a scant number of jobs? I was a starving artist, literally—starving for a bowl of butter beans and a biscuit, some collard greens and fatback. There was nothing like it for sustaining the soul. I finally recognized that I needed to reconnect. I wanted my drawl back. I realized that family is important. Remeeting and embracing people restored me.

But what to do? I had different meaningless jobs and eventually found that I needed to leave again. I went to Washington, D.C., which was the perfect middle ground to start anew. This time, I thought I should leave a biscuit trail so I would have an easier time finding my way back. I decided to spend a lot of money to learn how to cook—something I'm sure my grandmother would have taught me for free, but that would have been too easy. I went to culinary school and discovered I had a love of the preparation of food. I loved to cook—who knew?

I also discovered I was a bit squeamish and not very adventurous about food. In culinary school, the chef/instructor prepared beef tartare for us to taste. Hmm, let me see, seasoned raw beef with a raw egg in it. No thanks! Later that day came the offal chapter—kidney, liver, sweetbreads, etc. I again shook my head. Hell no! I did not get a good grade that day.

Some of what I learned in culinary school has been helpful, but I believe a large part of it involved how to be "bougie"—that's urban speak for aspiring to be a higher class than one is. For years, I did this in different types of establishments. In more than one place, my job was to bring newly graduated culinarians into the real world of cooking and restaurants. My job was essentially to make them cry. I did my job well—still do.

Eventually, my partner, Vivián, and I came back to Winston-Salem. We wanted to open a place that offered great food celebrating our Southern heritage. But it bothered us that people naturally assumed that when two African-American women opened a restaurant—especially one called Sweet Potatoes—it had to be a soul food place. I had a picture of what soul food restaurants looked like—the cafés and diners of my childhood—and that was not our vision. We wanted a restaurant, not a café. We wanted to serve Southern food, not soul food.

Right before we opened Sweet Potatoes, I visited a local cafeteria that treaded that boundary of soul/Southern/comfort food. I went through the line and ordered. It was good-looking food until the server put it on my plate.

A big plop of mashed potatoes—too much for the plate—overrun with gravy. A small single-serving bowl (what restaurants call a "monkey dish") overflowing with greens. And the biggest fried chicken breast I had ever seen. All on one plate, which was too small to hold it all. Capping it off was iced tea so sweet I still get a toothache just thinking about it. I actually could not eat until I cleaned the rim and side of my plate. The food was good, but we opened our restaurant with the notion that this was not what we wanted. Ironically, the cafeteria, which had operated for what seemed like a hundred years, recently closed. I suppose its demise was the product of the economy, or maybe just people's addiction to the Food Network.

We made our dream a reality when we opened Sweet Potatoes in January 2003. I had always compared soul food to the fighter George Foreman, who would stand there flatfooted and go toe to toe. The way he fought wasn't pretty or fancy, but he got the job done. On the other hand, my vision of Southern food was like Muhammad Ali—a little prettier, with fancier footwork. But the results were the same. I missed the connection that they were both great fighters. Once I got off my high horse, I starting wanting to expand by culinary point of view. But how do you make what is essentially castoff food into a "cuisine"?

I grew interested in learning about the history of soul food. Pig tails, neck bones, pig ears, and pigs' feet sound like they belong in the trash can at a pig farm, but this was the kind of food that was left for the slaves to eat. During the difficult times of Reconstruction and through the Depression, blacks and whites in the South often ate the same things, including the castaway parts of hogs. The division came when the white population prospered and the black population did not. The blacks still had to make a lot from a little, which was not an easy task. It takes time to "romance" the flavor from bitter greens. It takes time and effort to make the least cuts of meat not just tender but tasty. It's an enviable talent—one that should not be dismissed so readily.

I came to realize that this food is part of our history and deserves respect. In the 1970s, there was a genre called "blaxploitation" films because they perpetuated common white stereotypes about black people. Blacks bought into that term and mocked those films, or at least allowed others to do so. In some ways, the same thing happened to soul food. We were told soul food was bad for us, that it was holding us back. Now, I acknowledge that some of what we call soul food shouldn't be eaten every day. I also know a lot of other foods—Big Macs, Whoppers, and the like—that we shouldn't eat every day

either. The irony is that our ancestors raised and prepared foods with little processing or chemicals. A fatback biscuit after you plowed the fields, picked the cotton, or worked a sixteen-hour day in the factory kept you going. Just as the blaxploitation films allowed talented black folk to make a living working in a closed industry, soul food sustained us when money for food was tight.

My grandmother used to call finishing a good meal "getting the wrinkles out of our bellies." Nowadays, we've become lazy and privileged. We've lost sight of where we came from. Soul food gave us the pride and the ability to feed ourselves not hand to mouth, but heart to mouth. We learned to feed ourselves by any means necessary, and we fed ourselves from the soul. I have learned to cook, eat, be proud, and keep evolving.

In talking to people, I have learned there is a murky line between Southern and soul. Ernest Matthew Mickler, who wrote *White Trash Cooking*, said the difference between white trash and soul is that soul food is more highly seasoned. That may be true, but it is all survival cuisine. I suppose all food you're not afraid to share even if it's not plentiful, or food that comforts and nourishes more than the body is soul food of some sort.

From sunrise to sunset and every time in between, we celebrate with food. Food is the thing that brings us together. I may not know exactly what constitutes soul food, but I know the power of food. My connection to my grandmother is still food. Every time I fry chicken or prepare banana pudding, I feel a sense of pride that I learned an appreciation of food from her.

I know that the smothered pork chops I ate at a little place in Chapel Hill, North Carolina, called Walt's Grill were simple and delicious. But more than that, the place exuded a make-yourself-at-home feeling. When I walked into the place, a man laid a twenty-dollar bill on my table and said, "Welcome, and get yourself something to eat." Another man offered me a piece of fatback from his plate. I took it and ate it, though we were total strangers. It was all about community.

Sharon at the Tater Bread Café down the road in Durham shared the way she made collard greens and cabbage meet in the pot with one accord. I also know that I like the word *sopping* when it comes to biscuits and molasses at Mama Dip's in Chapel Hill. I know that *the* best chocolate cake is at Meta's in Winston-Salem. All of these places serve good food, whether you call it Southern or soul food. But more importantly, they all exhibit soul in their sense of community.

We've tried to establish that same sense of community—that *soul*—at

Walt's Grill, Chapel Hill

A gesture of community at Walt's Grill

Walt's pork chops

Tater Bread Café, Durham

7

Sweet Potatoes. Sweet Potatoes represents a melding of flavors—North and South, black and white, old and new. That's the soul in the food. Part of my odyssey has been learning that a chef is not any better than a cook in a café. I paid all sorts of money to get a culinary education and learn to be creative, but I don't think I actually *learned* how to cook. In my head, soul food required a cook, not a chef. There is book learning and common-sense learning. My most treasured and useful learning was from my grandmother and others like her, who cooked in cafés and grills. I learned from my mom and everyday people who fed their families on a little—the descendants of slaves who kept themselves alive on next to nothing. There is great talent to that. It's okay to know the correct culinary terms and how to create beautiful plates and grand presentations. I've never made a choice between style and substance. But for a long time, I constantly made the distinction between Southern and soul. Now, I've come to the conclusion that . . . *whatever*.

In this book, I share some of the things I've learned during my odyssey. Some of the recipes show you how to cook the leftover parts of a hog; some just show you how to make a tasty, filling meal out of very little. I've learned how to make entrails and feet and tails taste delicious. I've also learned how to make beans and greens more than just groceries.

Sweet Potatoes is a restaurant with a bar, a wine list, and servers. But our Smothered Pork Chops and Fried Chicken should taste just as good as those at Walt's Grill or Sylvia's. It just has to be done our way—the Sweet Potatoes way, with a side of soul.

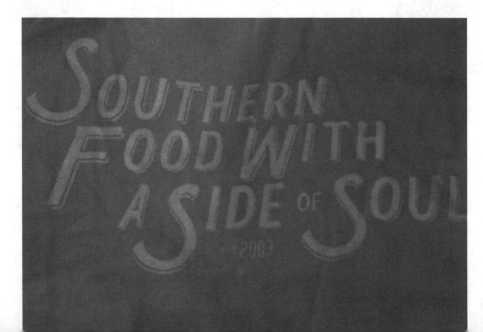

CHAPTER 1

THE SOULFUL PIG

FROM THE ROOTER TO THE TOOTER

I used to be a vegetarian, many years ago. Once while I was eating a big meat sandwich, someone made a comment about meat processing. It was not an encouraging or kind comment. It was just disgusting and a little scary. I didn't even bother to research the facts. I just put down the sandwich and did not eat any meat for six years. My recovery (no offense) came with something simple—the smell of country ham frying and the sight of a biscuit beside it. Have mercy—I was back!

I have a history with pork. My grandmother's step-father raised a few pigs right in the city. I guess pigs don't need a lot of roaming room—just enough room to eat and . . . you know. Very little is wasted from the pig. I have learned that I have so much more pork to explore—from the lean to the mean.

SO MUCH PORK TO EXPLORE . . .

PorK
Neck-Bone
$1.29

MR. WILLIE'S CHITTERLINGS

FRIED CHITTERLINGS

FRIED CHITTERLINGS AND MUSTARD GREEN SALAD

C-LOAF AND SPAGHETTI WITH COLLARD GREEN PESTO

PIGS' FEET

GRILLED BBQ'D PIGS' FEET

NECK BONES AND PIG TAILS

SMOTHERED PORK CHOPS

FRIED PORK CHOP SANDWICH

SHERRY HANNAH'S ABSOLUTELY FABULOUS HAM

COUNTRY HAM WITH MOLASSES-DIJON MUSTARD GLAZE

COUNTRY HAM WITH RED-EYE GRAVY OVER CREAMY
GRITS

SLAP YO' MAMMA! BBQ SPARE RIBS

BRAISED COUNTRY RIBS WITH SMOKED SAUSAGE AND
SAUERKRAUT

SLOW COOKER BOSTON BUTT (PORK SHOULDER)

FATBACK

FRIED HOG JOWLS

Mr. Willie's Chitterlings

SERVES 4 OR 5

I'm starting with the tooter.

I am amazed at all the foods I have not cooked. I've never made any Asian dishes to speak of. I could probably figure out how to roll a drunk quicker than I could learn to roll an eggroll or sushi. Much the same with Wiener schnitzel. I've eaten it but never made it. My thoughts are that someday I will. Similarly, I'd never cooked chitterlings (or is it chitlins?). My thoughts on that were, *And I never will!* I was ashamed, ashamed, ashamed!

They are the quintessential soul food, part of the Southern tradition of making the most out of nothing. Finally, I was given the opportunity to learn why they smell (although I had a fair idea!), how to clean them, how to cook them, and (according to my sous chef, Willie, and my grandmother) why you don't eat just anybody's chitlins. Show me the chitlins!

Chitterlings are the small intestines of the pig, which brings to mind an old joke. A guy makes chitlins for his friend. The friend says, "These are good, but I liked the ones I had the last time with the corn and stuff in them." They *really* need to be cleaned.

Unless you just slaughtered a hog, chitterlings usually come frozen in five-pound blocks or ten-pound buckets. Once you thaw them, cleaning them thoroughly will take some time. It's tedious but very important and worth it. I emphasize that chitterlings are the intestines of the pig. Take your time. Pigs eat everything. If it looks like it's not supposed to be there—straw, corn, hair—remove it. Cleaning under warm running water is helpful. Clean, rinse, clean, rinse. Turn the intestines inside out. Remove any fat because there may be soil underneath it. Clean them well and they won't smell. (Hey, it rhymes!)

Chitterlings are usually cooked with hog maws (the lining of the pig's stomach). Hog maws take longer to cook, so start them first.

Willie Smith has been my sous chef for a number of years. He is a serious old-school cook who came up through the ranks. He is big on the pig and showed me the way of chitterlings. I'm still recovering from it.

2 pounds hog maws, washed and cut

1 onion

3 quarts water

1 beef bouillon cube

1 chicken bouillon cube

1 tablespoon crushed red pepper flakes

2 teaspoons salt

2 teaspoons pepper

10 pounds chitterlings, cleaned and cut into 1-inch pieces

Place the hog maws in a pot with all the remaining ingredients except the chitterlings. Bring to a boil, then reduce to a simmer. Cook for 2 hours and add the chitterlings. Cook an additional 2 to 3 hours covered until tender.

Note C-Loaf is a good hog-maws shortcut. It's cooked and seasoned and has just a little chitterlings and a lot of maws. Add it at the end of your chitterling-cooking process.

Serving Suggestions

A bottle of Texas Pete
Skillet Cornbread (see page 107)
Spicy Collard Greens (see page 71)
Ms. Ora's Down-Home Tater Salad (see page 95)

Gertrude's Mac and Cheese (see page 89)

Fried Chitterlings

SERVES 6

If your intention is simply to fry the chitterlings, *clean them well.* Using the previous Chitterlings recipe minus the maws, cook then drain.

1 cup flour

1 egg beaten with 2 tablespoons water

2 cups seasoned breadcrumbs

2 pounds chitterlings, cleaned, cooked, and cut into 1- to 2-inch pieces

2 to 3 cups vegetable oil for frying

Place flour, egg wash, and breadcrumbs into 3 separate bowls. Dip the chitterlings in small batches in the flour, then the egg wash, then the breadcrumbs. Lay chitterlings on a lined plate. Pour oil into a large skillet or a cast-iron frying pan; oil should be halfway up the pan. Fry chitterlings in hot oil until golden brown.

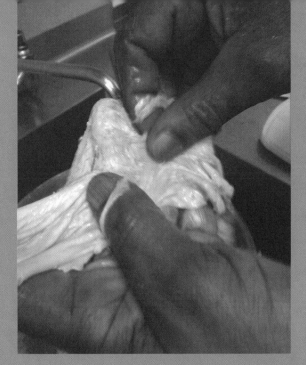

Cleaning chitterlings

*Chitterlings with Greens
and Macaroni and Cheese*

Fried Chitterlings and Mustard Green Salad

SERVES 4

2 pounds mustard greens, cleaned and chopped
½ cup diced tomatoes
4 cups Fried Chitterlings (recipe page 14)
shredded Parmesan cheese for garnish

Place the mustard greens in a large mixing bowl. Add the diced tomatoes and ¼ cup Apple Cider Vinaigrette (recipe below). Mix well. Divide the salad among 4 plates and top each with Fried Chitterlings. Garnish with Parmesan.

Apple Cider Vinaigrette

1 cup apple cider vinegar
2 tablespoons Dijon mustard
1 tablespoon honey
2 or 3 shakes Texas Pete
2 cups extra-virgin olive oil
salt and pepper to taste

In a medium-sized mixing bowl, add the vinegar, mustard, honey, and Texas Pete. Slowly whisk in the olive oil until well incorporated. Season with salt and pepper.

C-Loaf and Spaghetti with Collard Green Pesto

C-Loaf and Spaghetti with Collard Green Pesto

SERVES 4

I know I'm a little slow and out of touch, having just recently discovered C-Loaf—a loaf of chitterlings. It seems to be mostly maws but is really flavorful and certainly convenient, if you have a taste for chitterlings but not the inclination to clean and cook them. This recipe is an interesting way to enjoy your C-Loaf. A surprising number of folk like to eat chitterlings with spaghetti. Back in the seventies, there was an actual advertisement with a recipe in *Ebony* magazine—by Kraft (really!). I wonder what demographic they were trying to reach. Try this version.

1-pound package of your favorite C-loaf
1 cup water or beef or chicken stock
½ pound spaghetti
Parmesan cheese for garnish
hot sauce

Place the C-Loaf and water or stock in a medium saucepan. Bring to a boil, then reduce to a simmer. Cook for about 45 minutes until fork-tender. Cook spaghetti according to package directions and drain. Place in a bowl and toss with ¾ cup Collard Green Pesto (recipe below). To serve, place the pasta on a platter and spoon C-loaf in the center. Sprinkle with Parmesan and, of course, hot sauce.

Collard Green Pesto

4 cups firmly packed cleaned and chopped collard greens
¼ cup fresh basil
¼ cup Parmesan cheese
¼ cup toasted pecans
1 teaspoon Sriracha or your favorite Sriracha-type sauce
2 tablespoons apple cider vinegar
½ cup extra-virgin olive oil
1 teaspoon salt
1 teaspoon sugar

In the bowl of a food processor, place all ingredients except for the olive oil, salt, and sugar. Purée until smooth. With the motor running, slowly add the olive oil. Pulse in the salt and sugar.

Collard Green Pesto

Pigs' Feet

The techniques for cooking the tougher cuts of anything are low and slow, so as to tenderize and extract much flavor. Once the cooking is done, the enhancements come in.

4 pigs' feet, split
1 onion, diced
2 stalks celery, chopped
3 whole cloves garlic
1 cup apple cider vinegar
2 teaspoons crushed red pepper
flakes
2 tablespoons salt
2 teaspoons pepper
2 bay leaves

Clean the pigs' feet thoroughly under cold running water, removing any hair (with a disposable razor, if necessary). In a stockpot large enough to hold the pigs' feet, add enough water to cover by 4 inches. Add the remaining ingredients and bring to a boil. Skim the surface throughout the cooking process. Reduce the heat to a simmer and cook until the pigs' feet just start to get tender; you don't want them falling off the bone yet. If you are not going to add BBQ sauce, finish until they are tender and grab a bottle of hot sauce and some potato salad.

Grilled BBQ'd Pigs' Feet

SERVES 8

Follow the above recipe for Pigs' Feet. Remove the feet from the broth. Prepare a grill to medium heat. Place the Pigs' Feet cut side down. Baste with your favorite BBQ sauce (or the sauce on page 29). Grill for 15 minutes and turn over, basting the other side. Grill until the sauce is set and the pigs' feet are very tender.

Pigs' Feet with Greens and Potato Salad

If you'd rather use the oven, preheat to 350 degrees. Place the Pigs' Feet on a sheet tray and coat with the sauce. Bake for 15 minutes. Reduce the temperature to 325 degrees and bake an additional 20 to 30 minutes until the Pigs' Feet are tender and the sauce is set.

Note As an experiment, I soaked the cooked Pigs' Feet in buttermilk, coated them with seasoned flour, and fried them. They weren't bad, and I liked the texture better. Maybe we'll sell them at the fair next year!

Neck Bones and Pig Tails

SERVES 4 OR 5

You won't find a lot of meat or fat on the neck bones. And because fat is flavor, you'll need to enhance the flavor with something. This recipe uses pig tails, which add lots of flavor plus additional meat.

3 to 4 pounds neck bones
1 pound pig tails
3 stalks celery, chopped
1 large onion, diced
2 whole cloves garlic
1 tablespoon dried thyme
2 bay leaves
2 or 3 chicken or beef bouillon cubes
2 teaspoons salt
2 teaspoons pepper

Place the neck bones and pig tails in a large pot with water. Bring to a boil and cook for 20 minutes. This brings the scum to the surface. Remove the pot and rinse pot and meat. Return the meat to the pot and add enough water to cover. Add the remaining ingredients and bring to a boil. Cover, reduce to a simmer, and cook for 1½ to 2 hours until very tender.

Gravy

½ cup flour
¼ cup butter or oil
2 cups liquid from neck bones

Add the flour to a saucepan and cook until it starts to brown, being careful not to burn. Add the butter or oil. Stir until the mixture forms a smooth paste. Strain at least 2 cups of the liquid from the neck bones and stir it into the flour mixture. (The delicate crowd may prefer to remove the meat from the bones and add it to the gravy. Personally, I like sucking the bones.) Pour the gravy over the neck bones and pig tails. Serve with rice.

Smothered Pork Chops

SERVES 4

Smothered is a term used especially for meats that have been floured and browned, to which stock or water has been added, and that are simmered until tender. In one pot, you get meat and gravy! All you need is rice or potatoes.

½ cup vegetable oil
4 good-sized bone-in pork chops
½ teaspoon salt
½ teaspoon pepper
¼ teaspoon dried thyme
¼ teaspoon garlic powder
¼ teaspoon onion powder
1 cup all-purpose flour
1 medium onion, sliced
2 cups water or beef or chicken stock

Heat the vegetable oil in a large skillet. Season the pork chops with salt and pepper. Add the thyme, garlic powder, and onion powder to the flour; reserve 3 tablespoons of the flour mixture.

Dredge the chops in the flour mixture. Add the chops to the skillet and brown 2 to 3 minutes on each side. Remove the chops to a plate. Add the onions and cook until golden brown. Add the reserved flour mixture to the skillet and cook 2 minutes. Add the stock and bring to a boil. Reduce heat to a simmer and return the chops to the skillet. Cover and cook for 20 to 30 minutes until chops are tender and gravy has thickened.

Fried Pork Chop Sandwich

SERVES 4

The bones add flavor the way bones in fish add flavor. But I believe it's a lot easier to eat a bone-in pork chop sandwich than a bone-in fish sandwich!

4 bone-in pork chops
1 teaspoon salt
1 teaspoon pepper
1½ cups all-purpose flour
vegetable oil for frying
mayonnaise
mustard
8 slices white bread
Texas Pete

Season the pork chops with a little salt and pepper. Add 1 teaspoon each of salt and pepper to the flour. Heat about ½ inch of oil in a large skillet. Dredge the chops in the seasoned flour. When the oil is hot, place chops in a single layer in the skillet. Fry for 3 to 4 minutes, then turn the chops over and fry an additional 3 minutes until golden brown and cooked through. Remove the chops and drain on a paper towel. Spread mayonnaise and mustard on 1 side of a slice of bread. Place a chop on top, add as much Texas Pete as you can stand, and top with another slice of bread. Repeat with remaining 3 chops. Serve with strawberry Kool-Aid or a glass of Pinot Grigio.

Sherry Hannah's Absolutely Fabulous Ham

SERVES
8 TO 10

Sherry is one of Vivián's favorite cousins. She does this recipe at family functions and has for years. This is a feat, as she does not eat pork. But I like her anyway—as well as this ham recipe. Sherry is adamant: *Do not overcook the ham!* Sometimes, cooking isn't recipes, but rather a way of doing things—technique. Our good friend Wanda Harrison in Washington, D.C., is what I would deem a "maverick" cook. She does things her way and has a magic touch with food. Unlike Sherry, Wanda injects her ham with pineapple and brown sugar, adds cloves, and then bakes it in 7UP. It's all about the end result—*flavor!*

6- to 7-pound ham, whole or spiral
2-liter bottle ginger ale
20-ounce can sliced pineapple
10-ounce jar maraschino cherries
whole cloves

Preheat oven to 350 degrees. Line a large glass baking pan with aluminum foil. Place the ham in the pan fatty side up. Using a sharp knife, cut small slits into the ham. Pour half the ginger ale over the ham. Mix half the juice from the pineapple with half the syrup from the cherries and pour over ham. Stick cloves in the slits—*lots of cloves!* Baste the ham with the juices, cover with foil, and bake for about 20 minutes per pound. Baste often.

Twenty minutes before the end of the cooking time, remove the ham from the oven. Remove the foil, place pineapple slices on the ham, and put a cherry in the center of each slice,

Sherry Hannah's
Absolutely Fabulous Ham

attaching them with toothpicks. Pour the glaze (recipe below) over the fruit. Place the ham back in the oven uncovered and continue to bake for 15 to 20 minutes until glaze is set.

Glaze

1 cup dark brown sugar
1 cup light brown sugar
honey to taste

Mix the dark and light brown sugar in a medium bowl. Add the remaining pineapple and cherry juices and stir in honey. Add any juices from the ham to get a thick enough glaze to cover the ham.

Country Ham with Molasses–Dijon Mustard Glaze

SERVES
20 TO 25

I am a big fan of country ham. I don't prepare it often because it's a little time consuming to do a whole ham, and then there's the salt factor. Soaking the ham helps, but it's country ham—that's what makes it different from city ham, which is usually injected with water to keep it moist. Country ham is, well, hammier! And it offers the added bonus of a great bone left over for soups. I've even done Cheerwine soda as a glaze for country ham. Here, I use Molasses–Dijon Mustard Glaze.

13- to 14-pound country ham
2 cups apple cider
½ cup apple cider vinegar

Scrub the ham under running water. Use a stiff brush to remove any mold or cure. Place the ham in a container large enough to hold it. Fill the container with cold water and soak the ham for at least 2 days, changing the water every day.

Country Hams

After soaking, place the ham in a large roaster skin side up. Add the cider and cider vinegar and enough water to come ¾ of the way up the ham. Cover the ham with foil, place it in a 325-degree over, and bake for 3 to 3½ hours until the internal temperature reaches 155 degrees. Remove the ham from the oven and allow it to cool enough to handle. Remove the rind from the ham and leave at least ¼ inch of fat. Coat the ham with the glaze (recipe below). Raise the temperature of the oven to 375 degrees. Return the ham to the oven uncovered for an additional 25 to 30 minutes. Baste with the glaze every 15 minutes. Be careful not to burn the glaze. Remove the ham from the oven and let it sit for 20 minutes before slicing.

Note Slices of country ham are convenient and quick. There is nothing like waking up to the smell of country ham frying in the morning.

Molasses–Dijon Mustard Glaze

1 cup Dijon mustard
2 cups molasses
¼ teaspoon cayenne pepper
¼ teaspoon ground cloves

Combine the ingredients in a small bowl.

Country Ham with Red-Eye Gravy over Creamy Grits

SERVES 4

Creamy Grits

2 cups heavy cream
2 cups water
1 tablespoon salt
1 cup stone-ground grits

In a heavy saucepan, heat the cream, water, and salt to a boil. Slowly add the grits. Simmer uncovered for 30 to 45 minutes until the grits are creamy and no longer crunchy.

Country Ham with Red-Eye Gravy

2 tablespoons oil or bacon grease
4 slices center-cut country ham, ¼ inch thick
2 teaspoons sugar
1 cup black coffee
2 tablespoons unsalted butter

Heat oil or bacon grease in a large skillet. Add the ham and cook until brown; do in batches if necessary to cook in 1 layer. Sprinkle the ham with sugar and turn when ham is brown. Remove the ham from the skillet. Add the coffee to the skillet and simmer for 2 to 3 minutes. Add the butter and stir until sauce is smooth and butter has melted. Serve over ham and grits.

Slap Yo' Mamma! BBQ Spare Ribs

SERVES 8

So it's the middle of January and two degrees outside, but you want BBQ ribs and you really don't want to go to your grill and put the ribs on for three to four hours and freeze your hiney off. The solution? Use the oven in your nice warm kitchen. The results taste pretty darn good!

Rib Rub   Yields a little over 1½ cups

¼ cup salt
¼ cup pepper
2 tablespoons granulated garlic
2 tablespoons dried thyme
1 tablespoon dried mustard
3 tablespoons smoked paprika
1 tablespoon onion powder
½ cup light brown sugar

Combine all ingredients. Store unused portion in an airtight container.

Ribs

4 pounds spare ribs
2 cups Seriously Good BBQ Sauce (recipe on next page) or your favorite BBQ sauce

To prepare the ribs, remove the membrane from the back of the rack with a sharp knife. Coat the ribs with a generous amount of the rub. Line a baking pan with foil. Place the ribs in the pan, cover with foil, and roast at 300 degrees for 3 to 4 hours until tender. Remove from the oven and brush with half of the BBQ sauce, then return to the oven uncovered. Turn the temperature to 400 degrees and roast an additional 15 to 20 minutes to set the sauce. Brush with more sauce before serving.

Seriously Good BBQ Sauce

1 tablespoon olive oil or vegetable oil
½ cup diced yellow onion
1 teaspoon cumin
1 teaspoon allspice
pinch of cloves
3 cups ketchup
⅓ cup Worcestershire sauce
½ cup molasses
1 teaspoon salt
1 teaspoon pepper
1 teaspoon Liquid Smoke

Heat the oil in a medium-sized heavy saucepan. Add the onions and cook about 6 minutes until onions start to brown. Add the cumin, allspice, and cloves and cook 1 to 2 minutes more. Add the remaining ingredients and simmer for 20 minutes until the sauce thickens. Allow sauce to cool.

Ribs, cabbage,
stewed tomatoes and okra

Braised Country Ribs with Smoked Sausage and Sauerkraut

SERVES 6 TO 8

They're not actually ribs—closer to pork chops, but cut from the shoulder. You can braise them or grill them—very versatile.

vegetable oil
4 pounds country ribs
salt and pepper to taste
1 large onion, sliced
1 cup white wine
2 cups low-sodium chicken broth
32-ounce jar sauerkraut
2 pounds smoked sausage (such as Roger Wood), cut in half
2 teaspoons sugar

In a Dutch oven, add enough oil to coat the bottom of the pan. Season the ribs with salt and pepper. Brown the ribs on all sides and remove to a plate. Add the onions to the pan and cook 5 to 6 minutes until soft and lightly browned. Deglaze the pan with the white wine, scraping up the brown bits. Add the broth and bring to a boil. Lower the heat to a simmer and add the pork chops, any accumulated liquid, and the sauerkraut. Cover, place in a 350-degree oven, and cook for 1½ hours. Remove the pan from the oven and add the sausage and sugar. Cover, return to the oven, and continue to cook for about 45 minutes until the ribs are very tender. Adjust seasoning.

Pork, sauerkraut, and pinto beans! I'm just saying . . .

Slow Cooker Boston Butt (Pork Shoulder)

SERVES 6

This is a great no-fuss way to pulled-pork BBQ. Those who swear by the smoker will cringe, but everybody doesn't have time for that! Start this in the morning before you leave for work, and by the time you get home all you'll need are buns and some slaw.

1 onion, cut in half
4- to 5-pound Boston butt
½ cup spicy brown mustard
½ cup Rib Rub (see page 28)
1 cup apple cider vinegar
½ cup ketchup
½ cup water

Place the onion halves in the bottom of a crockpot. Trim the excess fat from the pork and coat the pork with the mustard. Cover liberally with Rib Rub. Add the vinegar, ketchup, and water to the pot and place the pork with the fattest side down on top of the onions. Cover and cook on low for 10 to 12 hours. Remove the very tender pork from the crockpot to a sheet tray and shred it with 2 forks. Return the pork to the crockpot and its accumulated juices and cook on high for an additional 30 minutes. Remove to a serving platter. Serve on soft buns with Creamy Coleslaw (see page 60), sliced red onion, and Texas Pete.

Fatback

SERVES 4

I wish that I could ever be
As svelte and graceful as Be-yon-cé.
I'm afraid that I will always lack
'Cause I got to have a biscuit, molasses, and fatback.
You know that I would never rest
If my eating were disrupted by Kanye West.

1 pound sliced fatback
3 cups water

Place the fatback and water in a medium saucepan. Bring to a boil and cook for 15 minutes. Drain and rinse the fatback. Dry on a paper towel. In a skillet large enough to hold the fatback in a single layer, fry over medium heat until lightly browned. Turn over and continue to cook for 10 to 12 minutes until crisp. Drain on a paper-towel-lined plate.

Why did you cook this? So you can have it in a biscuit with molasses and butter!

right: *Side meat*

Fried Hog Jowls

SERVES 4 OR 5

As with fatback, you can buy hog jowls sliced. It's great seasoning meat, but it's a must at New Year's, along with Hoppin' John. I actually prefer it to bacon or fatback. It's got a lot more flavor, especially on a sandwich with lettuce, tomato, and mayonnaise.

8 to 10 slices hog jowls

Lay the jowls in a single layer in a cast-iron frying pan or skillet. Fry over medium heat for about 7 minutes until the meat starts to brown. Turn the slices and continue to cook until crispy and brown (including the rind). Remove to a paper-towel-lined platter.

CHAPTER 2

SOUL MATES

CHICKEN, COW, AND THE FISHES IN THE SEA

I suppose my family, like many folk, ate a lot of chicken—*a lot*. It was inexpensive and versatile. And although we could stretch beef in meatloaf or Hamburger Helper or beef stew, it was still expensive, so we didn't have it often. And my mom could kill a steak or roast to the point that we would hide it in the cushions of our dining-room chairs, rather than eat it. Chicken and fish (sticks) were our friends.

FOOD IS THE
THING THAT
BRINGS US
TOGETHER . . .

FRIED CHICKEN

OVEN-"FRIED" BUTTERMILK CHICKEN

AIN'T NOTHING LIKE SPICY CHICKEN WINGS

COMPANY'S COMING ROAST CHICKEN AND VEGETABLES

EVERYDAY BBQ CHICKEN

STEWED CHICKEN AND RICE

FRIED CHICKEN LIVERS

SMOTHERED CHICKEN LIVERS

HOLIDAY ROAST TURKEY WITH CORNBREAD STUFFING
AND FRESH CRANBERRY AND ORANGE SAUCE

FRIED TURKEY

TURKEY HASH

SMOTHERED TURKEY WINGS x 2

STEPHANIE'S SLOW COOKER POT ROAST

BEEF SHORT RIBS

BEEF-A-RONI

LIVER AND ONIONS

CAROLINA CRAB CAKES

FISH FRY

LOW COUNTRY BOIL

BIG FRIED REAL SHRIMP

SALMON CROQUETTES

FRIED RICE, SALMON, AND EGGS

Fried Chicken

SERVES 4

Fried chicken is the peacemaker, the consoler, the celebrator. It's not just soulful, it's the heart of being Southern.

3-pound fryer, cut up
salt and pepper to taste
2 cups all-purpose flour
½ teaspoon salt
½ teaspoon pepper
2 tablespoons cornstarch
vegetable oil for frying (or some of the grease in the coffee can on the stove)
2 or 3 pieces fatback (optional)

Season the chicken with salt and pepper and allow to sit, covered, in the refrigerator for up to 1 day for the best flavor.

In a large bowl or plastic bag, combine the flour, salt, pepper, and cornstarch. Add the chicken and coat well. Add oil halfway up the side of a large (preferably cast-iron) skillet. Heat the oil and add the chicken pieces and fatback (if using). Fry the chicken in batches if need be, so as not to crowd the pan. Fry for about 10 minutes until it starts to brown. Adjust the flame to medium and turn the chicken. Continue to cook until chicken is golden brown, juices are no longer pink, and an instant-read thermometer inserted in the thickest part reads 165 to 170 degrees. Remove the chicken (and fatback) from the pan and drain on a paper-towel-covered platter.

Note Instant-read thermometers are available practically everywhere, including your neighborhood grocer. They're an invaluable tool in the kitchen.

Oven-"Fried" Buttermilk Chicken

SERVES 6

A tasty, healthier version. It's kind of like my favorite commercial growing up—"It's Shake 'N and Bake! And I helped!"

2 cups buttermilk
2 tablespoons olive oil
2 tablespoons Dijon mustard
1½ teaspoons kosher salt, divided
1½ teaspoons pepper, divided
6 boneless, skinless chicken breasts
2 cups cornflake crumbs or unseasoned breadcrumbs
¼ cup all-purpose flour
¼ teaspoon dried thyme
¼ teaspoon granulated garlic
¼ teaspoon paprika

Combine the buttermilk, olive oil, mustard, 1 teaspoon of the salt, and 1 teaspoon of the pepper in a mixing bowl. Add the chicken breasts, coat well, cover, and refrigerate for at least 1 hour. Preheat oven to 425 degrees. Place a wire rack on a rimmed baking sheet. Spray the rack with vegetable spray. Stir together the cornflake crumbs, flour, remaining salt, remaining pepper, and seasonings. Remove the chicken pieces and coat each thoroughly with the crumb mixture. Place the coated pieces on the rack and spray the chicken with vegetable spray. Bake for about 25 minutes until the chicken is golden brown and cooked through.

Ain't No Thing Like Spicy Chicken Wings

SERVES 4 OR 5

Who doesn't love good chicken wings? I like heat, but if you're a little shy, use a milder hot sauce.

½ teaspoon salt
½ teaspoon pepper
½ teaspoon granulated garlic
½ teaspoon smoked paprika
¼ cup vegetable oil
12 whole chicken wings

In a large bowl, combine the salt, pepper, garlic, paprika, and oil. Add the wings and toss to coat. Place the wings on a sheet tray and bake at 400 degrees for about 20 minutes until done. Remove the wings from the oven and brush well with glaze (recipe below). Return to the oven for 3 or 4 minutes to set the glaze. Serve with your favorite ranch or blue cheese dressing and sweet tea.

Have Mercy! Glaze

½ cup butter
2 tablespoons flour
½ cup extra-hot sauce (such as
   Texas Pete Hotter Hot Sauce)
½ cup orange marmalade

Combine the butter and flour in a small saucepan. Cook for 1 minute. Stir in the hot sauce and marmalade. Cook 3 to 4 minutes until thick.

Company's Coming Roast Chicken and Vegetables

SERVES 4 TO 6

It's not always fried.

5-pound roasting chicken
salt and pepper to taste
3 tablespoons butter
¼ cup chopped fresh herbs such as rosemary, thyme, sage, and/or parsley
2 teaspoons chopped garlic
1 lemon, cut in half

2 medium turnips, washed well and quartered
2 large carrots, peeled and cut into 2-inch pieces
1 sweet potato, peeled and diced medium
1 yellow onion, diced

Remove the giblets from the cavity and rinse the chicken. Season with salt and pepper inside and out. Carefully loosen the skin by gently running a finger underneath the skin of the breast and thigh area. In a small bowl, combine the butter, herbs, and garlic, mashing with your fingers. Place butter beneath the skin of the breast and distribute it evenly from breast to thigh. Place the lemon halves in the cavity of the chicken, then place chicken in a shallow roasting pan and roast uncov-

ered at 450 degrees for 20 minutes. Adjust the temperature to 375 degrees and roast another 20 minutes. Remove the chicken from the oven, add the vegetables to the pan around the chicken, and roast an additional 45 minutes to 1 hour until the juices run clear, the vegetables are done, and an instant-read thermometer registers 170 degrees. Remove from the oven and allow to rest for 15 minutes before carving.

A favorite 1-pot meal!

Everyday BBQ Chicken

SERVES 4 OR 5

4 or 5 chicken leg quarters
1 teaspoon salt
1 teaspoon pepper
favorite bottled BBQ sauce (or the sauce on page 29)

Preheat the oven to 400 degrees. Season the chicken with salt and pepper. Place the chicken pieces in a shallow baking pan and bake for 15 to 18 minutes. Remove from oven, brush with half of the BBQ sauce, and return to oven. Bake an additional 20 minutes

until the chicken is done. Baste with the remaining sauce halfway through the final cooking stage.

Note When you're having friends and family over for a cookout and want to throw a chicken on the grill, be sure to cook the bird first! Most people have no concept of how long it takes chicken to cook on the grill from raw. Save yourself a headache and some impatient guests. Cook the chicken in the oven, then finish it on the grill with the BBQ sauce. No burnt and raw chicken!

Stewed Chicken and Rice

SERVES 4 OR 5

1 teaspoon salt
1 teaspoon pepper
½ teaspoon dried thyme
¼ teaspoon savory
3-pound chicken, cut into pieces
1 cup all-purpose flour
3 tablespoons vegetable oil
2 to 3 stalks celery, diced
2 to 3 carrots, peeled and diced
1 medium yellow onion,
  chopped
1 teaspoon chopped garlic
1 bay leaf
5 cups stock or water
4 cups cooked rice

Combine the salt, pepper, thyme, and savory in a small dish. In a medium mixing bowl, season the chicken and add the flour. Heat the oil in a Dutch oven. Shake off the excess flour and brown the chicken in batches. Remove to a platter. Add the celery, carrots, and onions to the pot. Cook for 5 to 6 minutes. Add the garlic and cook 2 minutes more. Return the chicken to the pot, along with any accumulated juices. Add the bay leaf and stock. Bring the pot to a boil, then reduce the heat to low and cook for 25 to 30 minutes until chicken is cooked through and tender. Serve over hot rice.

Fried Chicken Livers

SERVES 3 OR 4

1 pound chicken livers
1 tablespoon hot sauce
2 cups buttermilk
2 cups all-purpose flour
2 teaspoons salt
1 teaspoon pepper
½ teaspoon granulated garlic
1 tablespoon cornstarch
pinch of nutmeg
1 cup vegetable oil

Clean the chicken livers of excess fat or any other weird little things that don't look right. Add the hot sauce to the buttermilk, then add the livers. Combine the flour with salt, pepper, garlic, cornstarch, and nutmeg in a large skillet. Add vegetable oil to about halfway up the skillet. Heat oil to 350 degrees (you'll know when you add a little bit of flour to the oil and it sizzles).

Coat the livers with the flour mixture; be prepared for the livers to pop something fierce when fried. Fry 3 to 4 minutes in batches, then drain on a paper towel. Serve hot with your favorite hot sauce (which should be Texas Pete).

Smothered Chicken Livers

Smothered Chicken Livers

SERVES 3 OR 4

2 tablespoons seasoned flour
2 cups chicken stock or broth

Prepare the recipe for Fried Chicken Livers on page 44. Drain all but about 2 tablespoons of the oil from the pan and add seasoned flour. Cook until lightly browned. Slowly add stock or broth to the pan. Bring to a boil, add chicken livers, and simmer for 4 to 5 minutes. Serve over rice or grits.

Holiday Roast Turkey with Cornbread Stuffing and Fresh Cranberry and Orange Sauce

SERVES 10

The first turkey I ever roasted, I searched the cavity for the bag of stuff and didn't find it. I roasted the turkey and found it later. I eased it out without anyone noticing and chalked it up to extra flavor. Trust me, it's in there. If not in the cavity, look for it tucked away at the head area of the bird.

12- to 14-pound turkey, giblets and neck reserved
salt and pepper to taste
4 tablespoons butter
2 tablespoons dried herbs (rosemary, thyme, sage)
1 teaspoon chopped garlic
1 orange, halved
fresh herbs (thyme, sage, rosemary)
2 cups low-sodium chicken broth or water

Remove the bag from the turkey. Rinse the turkey well inside and out. Remove any feathers and excess fat; you can use either tweezers or a lighter to remove fine feathers, especially on the wings and tail. Season the turkey inside and out with salt and pepper. Place the butter, dried herbs, and garlic in a small bowl and mash together until well combined. Gently loosen the skin of the breast and put the butter mixture underneath in the breast and thigh area. Add the orange halves to the cavity, along with the fresh herbs. Tie the legs of the turkey together with string and tuck the wing tips underneath the bird. Place the turkey in a roaster and add broth or water. Cover the turkey with foil and roast for 1 hour at 350 degrees. Remove the foil and continue to roast an additional 1 to 1½ hours, basting every 45 minutes until the turkey is done; the juices should run clear and an instant-read thermometer should register 180 degrees in the thickest part of the thigh and 165 degrees in the breast. Remove the turkey to a larger platter. Strain the drippings from the roasting pan. Skim off any fat.

Giblet Gravy

reserved giblets and neck
2 stalks celery, chopped
1 carrot, peeled and chopped
1 onion, chopped rough
3 cups turkey stock
3 tablespoons butter
3 tablespoons flour
salt and pepper to taste

Place the giblets and neck in a medium saucepan. Add the celery, carrots, and onions. Fill the saucepan halfway with water. Bring to a boil, then lower heat to a simmer. Cook on low for 1 to 1½ hours until the parts are tender. Strain the stock, removing the meat and discarding the vegetables. Combine strained stock with stock from the turkey for 3 cups of liquid. Finely chop giblets. Add the butter to a saucepan. Melt the butter over medium heat, then add the flour and cook until flour is light brown. Whisk in the reserved stock. Cook over medium heat until the gravy is thick and has no flour taste. Add the chopped giblets, along with any meat from the neck. Season with salt and pepper.

Cornbread Stuffing

¼ cup unsalted butter

2 cups diced yellow onion

2 cups diced green pepper

1 cup diced celery, green leafy
parts included

2 tablespoons rubbed sage

1 tablespoon dried thyme

2 tablespoons sausage seasoning (available from your favorite
butcher shop)

12 cups homemade Cornbread
(double batch of the recipe below), crumbled and toasted

2 or 3 green onions, chopped,
green parts only

½ cup chopped parsley

1 cup chicken or turkey stock

2 eggs, lightly beaten

In a large skillet, melt the butter and sauté the onions, peppers, celery, and seasonings until the vegetables are soft. Remove from heat. In a large mixing bowl, add the Cornbread crumbles (or cubes), green onions, and parsley. Add the sautéed vegetables and combine well. Stir in the stock and eggs. Place the dressing in a large buttered casserole or baking pan, cover with aluminum foil, and bake for 20 minutes at 350 degrees. Remove the foil and bake an additional 10 to 15 minutes until the dressing is firm and lightly browned.

Cornbread

1¼ cups white or yellow cornmeal

¾ cup all-purpose flour

⅓ cup sugar

1 tablespoon baking powder

½ teaspoon salt

1 cup milk

2 eggs, lightly beaten

¼ cup vegetable oil

In a medium mixing bowl, combine the cornmeal, flour, sugar, baking powder, and salt. In a separate bowl, mix together the milk, eggs, and oil. Add the wet ingredients to the dry. Do not overmix. Pour the batter into a greased 8-inch baking pan. Bake at 400 degrees for 20 to 25 minutes until the cornbread is golden brown and the center is firm when touched.

Cornbread stuffing

Fresh Cranberry and Orange Sauce

I know there's nothing like hearing the *thwok* of cranberry sauce coming out of the can and having a nice slice with the turkey, but . . .

1 cup sugar
½ cup orange juice
½ cup water
12-ounce bag cranberries
2 tablespoons orange zest

Combine the sugar, orange juice, and water in a saucepan. Bring to a boil. Rinse and pick through the cranberries, removing any stems and debris. Add the cranberries to the pot and simmer about 15 minutes until the cranberries burst. Stir in the orange zest. Remove the sauce from the heat and allow to cool before refrigerating. The sauce will continue to thicken as it cools.

Fried Turkey

SERVES 10

When did we start frying turkeys? I never had fried turkey growing up. Fried chicken, fried fish, but never turkey. I like the process of roasting a turkey—the smell, the drippings for making the gravy. You don't have that if you fry a turkey. But everyone I spoke with said, "Girl, once you've had fried turkey, that's the only way you'll want it." I figured, okay, I've got to at least try. I am a professional. Should be a cinch.

I had a turkey fryer I had purchased the previous summer for a fish fry. So I hadn't used the stuff that came with it, apparently meant for mounting and hoisting the turkey. I had no idea where this stuff was but eventually found it. I had bought a turkey on sale a few weeks early at a great price. It was solid as a rock, but I had a week to thaw it.

It is very important to follow the instructions. If not, bad things can happen. I found all sorts of videos about what can happen when fried turkeys go wrong. It even says on the turkey fryer that explosions and fires are possible. I take these warnings to heart, especially as I am not comfortable with propane.

Rule number one: You must not overfill the fryer. The instructions said to place the turkey in the empty fryer, fill it with water to cover, and then remove the turkey. That's the oil fill line. Unfortunately, my fill line was well beyond the line suggested by the manufacturer. The other question was how to season the turkey. Rub, injection, or both? I chose a rub and continued to be concerned about the fill line.

Oops. No oil. I forgot to buy oil, so off I went to the grocery store on Thanksgiving Day. Oh, look, turkeys on sale for half price! I thought I'd better get a backup turkey just in case things don't go well. I gathered my purchases and was on my way home with plenty of time to spare when, oops, I forgot the oil again. Dinner was at five, and it was almost two by then, so I rushed home and prepared the backup turkey for the oven. I planned to go back to the store, which closed in twenty minutes, though that would lose me more time. Then I had an *aha!* moment. I own a restaurant! With a fryer—

two fryers—and plenty of oil! It was Thanksgiving, and Sweet Potatoes wasn't open. Great idea!

Unfortunately, all great ideas are not good ideas. The fryer wasn't deep enough to completely submerge the turkey, so I had to keep turning it over with a pair of tongs and a spoon. It was very awkward. I burnt myself at least three times and actually overfried the turkey. Fortunately, I had a backup turkey roasting at home. Our guests were kind. I had lots of leftovers from the fried one.

I did fry a turkey again. In the turkey fryer. And it was the best turkey I've tasted. Very moist, crispy, and flavorful. Fried in the turkey fryer. Go figure. I might do one for Easter.

Note An eighteen-pound turkey is not a good fit for a turkey fryer. Less than fourteen pounds works better.

12- to 14-pound turkey
3 tablespoons Rib Rub (see page 28)
fryer oil (preferably peanut oil)

Prepare the turkey the day before. Remove the bag of giblets and neck from the cavity and rinse the turkey thoroughly. Dry with a paper towel and liberally season the turkey with the rub inside and out. Cover with plastic wrap and refrigerate overnight.

Remove the turkey from the refrigerator and allow to sit at room temperature for 30 minutes. Fill the fryer with oil according to the fryer instructions and heat to 350 degrees. This will take about 30 minutes. Carefully lower the turkey into the fryer. Allow 3 minutes per pound to reach an internal temperature of 165 degrees for the white meat and 170 degrees for the dark meat; this will take about 45 minutes. Drain on a paper-towel-lined sheet tray. Let stand for 15 to 20 minutes before carving.

SERVES 4 OR 5

I would almost roast a turkey just to have the hash. This is the best use I know for Thanksgiving leftovers (not counting leftover dressing and a little cranberry sauce for dinner or on toast with fried eggs for breakfast).

½ cup vegetable oil
½ cup chopped celery
1 medium onion, diced
1 green pepper, diced
1 teaspoon chopped garlic

2 teaspoons dried thyme
¼ cup flour
3 cups Homemade Turkey Stock
(recipe below)
4 cups light and dark turkey meat
picked from the bird, chopped
salt and pepper to taste

Heat the oil in a large skillet. Add the celery, onions, green peppers, garlic, and thyme. Cook over medium heat for about 5 minutes until the vegetables are soft. Stir in the flour and combine well. Slowly whisk in the stock until liquid is incorporated and sauce is smooth. Bring to a boil, then lower heat to a simmer. Add the turkey to the pan and simmer 4 to 5 minutes until heated through. Adjust the seasoning with salt and pepper.

Homemade Turkey Stock

When I was growing up, we used everything, including the bones. After you've gotten as much as you can from your turkey, add the bones to a large pot, then add . . .

2 carrots, chopped into ½-inch
pieces
1 onion, chopped
2 stalks celery with leaves,
chopped
1 bay leaf
2 or 3 springs fresh thyme
1 or 2 whole cloves garlic

Place all ingredients in a stockpot and add enough water to cover by 3 inches. Bring to a boil, then simmer for 30 to 40 minutes. Skim the surface for debris. Strain the stock, discarding the solids. Allow stock to cool.

Smothered Turkey Wings x 2

SERVES 5 OR 6

Use both smoked turkey and fresh turkey for a more intense flavor.

2 stalks celery with leaves, chopped

1 medium onion, chopped

2 whole cloves garlic

2 teaspoons salt

2 teaspoons pepper

2 teaspoons dried thyme

2 teaspoons poultry seasoning

4 fresh turkey wings

2 smoked turkey wings

½ cup water or chicken broth

¼ cup flour

2 cups Homemade Turkey Stock (see page 53)

In a baking pan large enough to hold the wings in 1 layer, add the celery, onions, and garlic. Combine the seasonings. Rinse the fresh turkey wings and clip the tips. Season the fresh wings and place them in a layer on top of the vegetables, along with the smoked wings. Pour the water or broth into the pan and cover with foil. Bake for about 2½ hours until the wings are cooked through and very tender. Remove pan from oven and allow it to sit uncovered for 10 minutes. Remove wings and arrange on a large platter. Strain the stock and keep it in a medium saucepan. Add flour to the pot and cook until flour starts to brown slightly. Slowly add the turkey stock to the pan and stir in the vegetables. Allow to simmer for 10 minutes, then pour over the wings. Serve with grits and greens. Yum!

Stephanie's Slow Cooker Pot Roast

SERVES 6 TO 8

Crockpots are great time-saving tools, but it takes time to build trust. I sometimes fret, "Did I turn the coffeepot off?" or "Did I leave the iron on?" And now I'm going to purposefully leave something cooking in my house unattended? It took awhile for me to stop wondering what would happen if the liquid cooked out of the pot. Take that leap of faith.

2½- to 3-pound beef chuck roast
2 tablespoons oil
salt and pepper to taste
2 stalks celery, chopped large
2 carrots, peeled and chopped large
1 onion, peeled and quartered
2 or 3 whole cloves garlic
2 tablespoons dried rosemary
2 tablespoons dried thyme
2 bay leaves
2 tablespoons tomato paste
1 bottle chocolate stout or other dark beer
2 cups beef stock

Rub the beef with oil and season all sides with salt and pepper. Place the vegetables and garlic in a crockpot and sprinkle with the herbs. Combine the tomato paste, stout, and beef stock. Brown the beef in a heavy skillet for 3 to 4 minutes on each side to form a nice crust. Place the meat on top of the vegetables and pour in the liquid. Cook on low for 8 to 10 hours. The meat should be melt-in-your-mouth tender at this point. And you were worried!

Beef Short Ribs

SERVES 6

Short ribs are a lot meatier and more tender than spare ribs. But just like spare ribs, pot roast, and beef stew, they require low and slow cooking.

4 pounds beef short ribs
1 teaspoon salt
1 teaspoon pepper
3 tablespoons vegetable oil
1 onion, julienned
2 teaspoons chopped garlic
¼ cup all-purpose flour
1 cup red wine
3 cups beef stock
½ pounds medium mushrooms, halved
2 sprigs fresh rosemary

Season the ribs with salt and pepper. In a Dutch oven, heat the oil and brown the ribs in batches, about 5 minutes per side. Remove ribs to a platter. Add the onions and cook 3 to 4 minutes until soft. Add the garlic and cook 1 minute more. Stir in the flour. Slowly stir in the wine and stock. Return the ribs to the pot, along with any accumulated juices. Bring to a boil, cover, then lower the heat. Simmer for 2 hours. Remove the lid and add the mushrooms and rosemary. Continue to simmer an additional ½ hour until the ribs are tender. Serve with Simple Mashed Potatoes (see page 92).

Beef-A-Roni

SERVES 6

My mom had us totally trained. We did not like steak or real fish. But anything with macaroni and/or hamburger made us happy. And it did not always come from the can. We were suitably impressed when she whipped this up for us.

1 pound ground beef
1 tablespoon vegetable oil
½ cup diced green pepper
½ cup diced yellow onion
1 teaspoon salt
1 teaspoon pepper
1 teaspoon granulated garlic
15-ounce can tomato sauce
6-ounce can tomato paste
2 cups beef broth
3 cups elbow macaroni
2 tablespoons butter
2 cups shredded cheddar cheese,
  divided

Add the ground beef and oil to a large skillet. Cook over medium heat until brown. Add the green peppers, onions, salt, pepper, and garlic. Cook until the vegetables are soft, then add tomato sauce, paste, and broth. Cook for 5 minutes to heat through and blend flavors. While the meat sauce is cooking, cook macaroni in salted water for 8 to 10 minutes until tender. Drain and toss with butter. Pour macaroni into a large casserole dish. Stir in beef mixture and 1 cup of the cheese and combine thoroughly. Top with remaining cheese. Bake uncovered for 20 to 25 minutes until the cheese is melted and bubbly.

Liver and Onions

SERVES 3 OR 4

I don't like liver, so I have always done my very best to make it not taste like liver. Soaking it in milk with a bay leaf makes it taste a little less intensely liver-y, and it fries better.

1 pound beef liver
2 cups milk
1 bay leaf
1 teaspoon salt
1 teaspoon pepper
½ teaspoon dried thyme
1 cup flour
½ cup vegetable oil
1 large onion, julienned
1½ cups beef broth
dash of Worcestershire sauce

In a shallow dish, add the liver, milk, bay leaf, salt, pepper, and thyme. Refrigerate for 20 minutes. Place flour in a medium bowl. Heat oil in a skillet. Remove the liver and dredge in flour. Shake off excess and carefully add liver to the skillet. Cook 3 to 4 minutes on each side until lightly browned. Remove the liver to a lined plate. Add the onions to the skillet and cook until they start to soften and get a little color. Add the broth and Worcestershire, then return the liver to the pan. Allow to simmer for 10 to 12 minutes until sauce thickens. Serve over rice.

Carolina Crab Cakes

3 tablespoons butter
½ cup finely chopped onion
½ cup diced celery
½ cup diced green pepper
1 teaspoon lemon juice
1 tablespoon chopped parsley
1 tablespoon Dijon mustard
1 teaspoon Old Bay seasoning
1 tablespoon Worcestershire sauce
2 eggs
1½ cups breadcrumbs, divided
1 pound lump crabmeat, picked
¼ cup oil
6 soft sandwich rolls

In a medium skillet, heat the butter and add onions, celery, and green peppers. Cook for about 5 minutes until the vegetables are soft. Remove from heat and set aside to cool. In a medium bowl, combine the lemon juice, parsley, Dijon, Old Bay, Worcestershire, eggs, and 1 cup of the breadcrumbs. Place the reserved breadcrumbs on a plate. Gently fold the crabmeat into the egg mixture, then form into ½-cup patties. Heat oil in a large skillet. Coat the crab cakes in the reserved breadcrumbs and add to hot skillet in a single layer, in batches if necessary. Cook for 4 to 5 minutes until brown, then turn and cook the other side an additional 3 to 4 minutes. Remove to a paper-towel-lined platter. Serve on soft rolls with lettuce, tomato, and a generous dollop of Herbed Tartar Sauce (page 59).

Herbed Tartar Sauce

2 cups mayonnaise
2 tablespoons pickle relish
1 tablespoon capers
1¾ teaspoons chopped fresh parsley
1½ teaspoons dill
1½ teaspoons oregano
1½ teaspoons basil
1¼ tablespoons tarragon
1½ teaspoons chopped garlic
1 teaspoon anchovy paste
2 or 3 good shakes Worcestershire
  sauce

Combine all ingredients in a medium mixing bowl. Mixture can be refrigerated in an airtight container for up to 2 weeks.

SERVES 8 TO 10

The first thing you'll need is—*fish!* I like whiting. You'll probably need about a half to three-quarters of a pound of fish per person. Since you're cooking outdoors, people are going to smell this, so you'll probably see some folks you didn't know you knew. Have extra. You'll need a good fryer, a good breader, and good stuff to go with the fish. Simple is best—coleslaw, tartar sauce, white bread, and corn on the cob.

8 pounds fish fillets (whiting, catfish, or flounder)
salt and pepper to taste
1½ gallons buttermilk
6 cups yellow cornmeal
2 cups flour
⅓ cup cornstarch
2 tablespoons salt
1 tablespoon granulated garlic
1 tablespoon dried thyme
2 tablespoons pepper
1 to 2 gallons oil

Cut fillets in half, place them in a large pan, and season with salt and pepper. Pour the buttermilk over the fish. Combine the cornmeal, flour, cornstarch, and seasonings in a separate shallow pan and mix well. Heat the oil in a fryer to 350 degrees. Dredge the fish in the cornmeal mixture and shake off the excess. Carefully put fish in the oil. Repeat with 3 or 4 more pieces of fish; don't overcrowd the fryer. Fry for 4 to 5 minutes. Fish should be crisp and golden brown. Remove the fish to a lined platter or pan. Serve immediately with Creamy Coleslaw (recipe below) and all the fixins!

Creamy Coleslaw

¼ cup mayonnaise
¼ cup sour cream
1 tablespoon white vinegar
2 tablespoons sugar
1 teaspoon salt
1 teaspoon pepper
1 teaspoon celery seed
1 green cabbage (about 1 pound),
   shredded
1 carrot, peeled and shredded
½ cup finely diced yellow onion
½ cup diced green pepper

In a large bowl, combine the first 7 ingredients and mix well. Add the cabbage, carrots, onions, and green peppers. Mix well. This is best if it's chilled before serving.

Low Country Boil

SERVES 12 TO 14

Vivián's family (her father's side) is from Hilton Head and Bluffton, South Carolina. There, a "Low Country boil" is like our fish fry, except no grease! It's good anyway. Certain members of the seafood-eating population enjoy picking crabs. I am not one of them. For me, it's a lot of work for a little bit of meat. I like crab legs because you can get them more readily than blue crabs, and they're not crawling everywhere.

5 pounds red potatoes, halved

1 large onion, peeled and quartered

4 quarts water

3 12-ounce bottles beer

1 cup shrimp boil or Old Bay seasoning

5 pounds fresh shucked corn, halved

5 pounds smoked sausage

5 pounds good-sized shrimp, unpeeled

5 pounds blue crabs or crab legs (optional)

In a large pot, add the potatoes, onions, water, beer, and shrimp boil or Old Bay. Bring to a boil. Cook for 6 minutes, then add the corn and sausage. Return to a boil and cook for about 7 minutes until the potatoes are tender. Add the shrimp and crab (if using) and cook for an additional 5 minutes until shrimp and crab are pink. Drain, place on a newspaper-lined table, and enjoy! On page 63 is a good cocktail sauce for shrimp dipping.

Easy Cocktail Sauce

2 cups ketchup
¼ cup prepared horseradish
2 tablespoons Key lime juice
1 tablespoon Worcestershire sauce
1 tablespoon Texas Pete
1 teaspoon pepper

Stir all ingredients together and refrigerate.

Big Fried Real Shrimp

Not those popcorn shrimp I had growing up!

2 to 3 cups vegetable oil
2 cups buttermilk
1 egg, lightly beaten
2 or 3 shakes hot sauce
2 pounds large shrimp, peeled and deveined
2 cups cornmeal
½ cup all-purpose flour
2 tablespoons cornstarch
2 tablespoons Old Bay seasoning

Heat at least 3 inches of oil in a large cast-iron skillet or Dutch oven. Combine the buttermilk, egg, and hot sauce in a bowl and add the shrimp. In a separate bowl, mix together the cornmeal, flour, cornstarch, and Old Bay. Dredge the shrimp in the cornmeal mixture and place on a sheet tray. Add the shrimp to the hot oil and fry in batches for about 2 minutes on each side until golden brown. Drain on a paper-towel-lined platter. Serve immediately.

Enhancements

Got to have Hush Puppies (see page 109)!
Creamy Coleslaw (see page 60)
Easy Cocktail Sauce (see page 63)

Salmon Croquettes

SERVES 8

My mom used canned salmon for croquettes. I don't think I actually saw a fresh salmon fillet until I was in my twenties. One pound of cooked salmon works for this recipe also.

14¾-ounce can salmon
½ cup diced onion
½ cup diced green pepper
2 teaspoons dill
2 eggs, beaten
1½ cups Italian breadcrumbs
¼ cup vegetable oil for frying

Place salmon (including liquid) in a medium bowl. Break apart salmon, including the bones. Mix in the onions, peppers, and dill. Fold in the eggs and breadcrumbs, then form into 8 patties. Heat the oil in a large skillet. Add the salmon patties and cook for 3 to 4 minutes, then turn over and fry on the other side until brown.

Fried Rice, Salmon, and Eggs

This has proven to be a breakfast (or dinner) of champions when there is little else in the house.

¼ cup vegetable oil or bacon grease
¼ cup diced onion
¼ cup diced green pepper
1 cup rice
2 cups water
14¾-ounce can salmon
2 eggs, beaten
salt and pepper to taste
Texas Pete to taste

In a large frying pan, heat the oil and add the onions and green peppers. Cook over medium heat until the vegetables are soft. Add the rice and cook for about 3 minutes until it browns slightly. Add the water and bring to a boil. Cover and lower the heat. Cook about 20 minutes until the rice is done. Remove the lid and stir in the salmon and eggs. Return the lid to the pan with the heat on low for 5 minutes. Remove the lid and fluff the egg/rice mixture. Season with salt and pepper and a little Texas Pete.

Note This is a great way to use leftover rice. Just heat the rice and stir in the eggs and salmon.

Enhancement

Cheese makes everything better! Top with grated cheese.

CHAPTER 3

VEGGIE SOUL

A lot of times, meat was just the added seasoning to vegetables or beans. I visited my grandmother once during the period when I didn't eat meat. I explained to her that I was a vegetarian, and she smiled and pointed to her pot on the stove and said, "Baby, these is vegetables." I looked into her pot filled with garden-fresh green beans and a big ham hock. I just smiled and got a plate of green beans.

Vegetables—whether fresh from the garden, canned, or frozen—are as important as the meat. Much care should be given to flavor. Veggies have always been an integral part of the meal. Sometimes, they were the meal.

"BABY, THESE IS

VEGETABLES . . ."

SPICY COLLARD GREENS

QUICK(ER) POT OF GREENS

SMOTHERED CABBAGE AND COLLARD GREENS

FRIED CABBAGE

GREEN BEANS COOKED IN THE WAY OF THE SOUTH
WITH WHITE POTATOES

BLACK-EYED PEAS

BAKED SWEET POTATOES

CANDIED SWEET POTATOES

OKRA FRITTERS

STEWED OKRA AND TOMATOES

CORN PUDDING

SUMMER'S BOUNTY SUCCOTASH

Spicy Collard Greens

SERVES 7 OR 8

These are my go-to greens. They stand up to a long cooking time because they're sturdy. There are two schools of thought—slightly crispy, or so tender you don't have to chew them. I like the latter.

8 to 10 cups chicken stock
2 tablespoons salt
1 pound smoked meat (ham hock or turkey)
1 tablespoon dried thyme
1 teaspoon crushed red pepper flakes, or to taste
1 large onion, chopped
5 pounds collard greens
butter or bacon grease
1 teaspoon sugar
2 tablespoons apple cider vinegar

Put stock and salt in a large pot and bring to a boil. Add the meat, thyme, red pepper, and onions. Cook over medium heat for about ½ hour to season the liquid. In the meantime, clean the greens. Wash in cold water and remove the tough stems with a chef's knife. Roll 5 or 6 leaves together and cut them into 1½-inch-wide strips. Rinse the greens with a bowl of salted water. Remove to a colander and repeat until the water is clear and free of sand. Add the cleaned greens to the simmering stock. Return the pot to a boil, then reduce to a simmer. Cook the greens for 45 minutes to 1 hour until tender. Finish the greens with butter or bacon grease, sugar, and vinegar.

Turnips and greens

Quick(er) Pot of Greens

SERVES 4 OR 5

Collards are the toughest of the greens. I'm not particularly fond of them alone. Cooking time is longer with collard greens. So, to be quick about it, I eliminate the collards and do a combo of turnip and mustard greens, with the addition of turnip root.

2 pounds greens (1 bag of pre-washed mixed greens or 1 bunch each of mustard, turnip, and kale)
2 tablespoons olive oil
4 to 6 strips bacon, chopped
1 yellow onion, diced
½ teaspoon crushed red pepper flakes
2 teaspoons chopped garlic
1 teaspoon dried thyme
2 cups chicken broth
1 pound turnip root, diced
salt and pepper to taste
vinegar to taste

If using bulk greens, trim, remove tough stems, and wash thoroughly. Heat the oil in a large pot and add bacon and onions. Cook until the fat has been rendered from the bacon and the onions are soft and starting to brown. Add the red pepper, garlic, and thyme. Cook for 1 to 2 minutes. Add the broth and bring to a boil. Add the greens and turnip root and return to a boil. Reduce heat to a simmer, cover, and cook for 20 to 25 minutes until tender. Add salt and pepper and vinegar. Serve hot with a pan of cornbread.

Smothered Cabbage and Collard Greens

SERVES 6 TO 8

2 tablespoons olive oil
4 strips bacon, chopped
1 yellow onion, chopped
2 cups chicken broth
14½-ounce can diced tomatoes
1 bunch collard greens, tough stems removed, cleaned and chopped
1 large head cabbage, cored and chopped
1 teaspoon sugar
1 teaspoon salt
1 teaspoon pepper
crushed red pepper flakes to taste

In a large pot or a Dutch oven, heat the oil and add bacon and onions. Cook until the onions are soft and starting to brown along with the bacon. Add the broth and tomatoes, including the juices. Bring to a boil. Add the collards, cover, and simmer for 15 minutes. Uncover, stir in the remaining ingredients, and cook on low for about 20 minutes until the greens and cabbage are tender.

Cabbage and greens

Fried Cabbage

SERVES 5 OR 6

I say "fried," but it's really just braised in its own juices. Bacon adds a smoky flavor. Olive oil and butter work well also, along with a little smoked paprika and salt and pepper for depth.

4 strips bacon, chopped
1 tablespoon butter
1 yellow onion, diced
1 large head green cabbage, chopped
2 teaspoons sugar
1 teaspoon salt
1 teaspoon pepper
1 teaspoon dried thyme
1 cup chicken stock
splash of apple cider vinegar (optional)

In a large pot or a Dutch oven, add the bacon and butter and cook until bacon is crisp. Add the onions and cook about 5 minutes until soft. Add the cabbage, sugar, salt, pepper, thyme, and stock. Cover and cook on low for 15 to 20 minutes until tender. Uncover and stir every 10 minutes of so. Add the vinegar, if desired. Cook an additional 5 minutes to blend flavors. Serve hot with cornbread!

Cabbage

Green Beans Cooked in the Way of the South with White Potatoes

I was talking to someone about how long they cook their green beans, and they said, "Around an hour and a half to two hours." I thought, *Wow, that's a long time for green beans*. Then I realized in further conversation that most of that time is spent seasoning the liquid with ham hocks, smoked turkey, or other seasoning meat.

1 pound ham hocks or smoked turkey
2 quarts water
1 yellow onion, sliced
2 teaspoons salt
1 teaspoon chopped garlic
2 pounds green beans or pole beans, trimmed and cut into 1½- to 2-inch pieces
1 pound new potatoes, peeled and quartered (if large) or halved (if small)
salt and pepper to taste

In a large pot, add the ham hocks or turkey and water. Bring to a boil, then reduce to a simmer for 1 hour. Add the onions, salt, garlic, beans, and potatoes and simmer about 20 minutes until tender. Adjust salt and pepper.

Black-Eyed Peas

SERVES 4 OR 5

I remember walking into the house one day as a child and seeing my father on the sofa shelling peas. It seemed odd for someone so totally masculine and stern. It made him less scary and more human. Shelling peas or beans and shucking corn are summer activities. I think everyone should do it; it's very Zen. This recipe uses dried beans. They're still good, even though someone else did the shelling for you.

2 or 3 strips bacon, chopped
1 tablespoon vegetable oil
½ cup diced green pepper
½ cup diced celery
1 cup diced yellow onion
1 teaspoon chopped garlic
1 pound black-eyed peas, picked
   and rinsed
6 cups water or chicken broth
2 teaspoons dried thyme
1 bay leaf
¼ teaspoon crushed red pepper
   flakes
2 teaspoons salt

In a Dutch oven or pot, cook the bacon in oil until it starts to brown. Add the green peppers, celery, onions, and garlic and cook until the vegetables soften. Add the peas, water or broth, thyme, bay leaf, and red pepper. Bring to a boil and simmer about 1 hour. Halfway through the cooking, add the salt. Continue to cook until the beans are tender. Drain and serve hot.

Baked Sweet Potatoes

SERVES 4

I am proud to say that North Carolina is the number-one producer of sweet potatoes in the United States. We do so much with sweet potatoes— fry them, boil them, mash them, put marshmallows on top—that we sometimes forget simple is best.

vegetable oil
4 medium sweet potatoes, washed well

Preheat the oven to 375 degrees. Lightly oil the potatoes and wrap them in foil. Place on a sheet tray and bake for 30 to 40 minutes until done. (They can also be microwaved in plastic wrap on high for 10 minutes.) Cut potatoes open and serve hot with butter and brown sugar or plain.

Enhancements

Chopped ham and melted cheese
Pineapple and ham
Coconut, pecans, and/or pineapple

Candied Sweet Potatoes

Delicious as a dessert or side, especially with ham.

8 medium sweet potatoes (about 5 pounds), peeled and sliced ¼ inch
4½ cups sugar
1 cup light brown sugar
2 teaspoons cinnamon
1 teaspoon nutmeg
3 teaspoons vanilla extract
3 teaspoons lemon extract
½ pound unsalted butter, cubed

Place a layer of sliced sweet potatoes in a large casserole dish or baking pan. In a medium mixing bowl, combine the sugar, brown sugar, cinnamon, and nutmeg. Cover the layer of sweet potatoes with ¼ of the sugar mixture. Sprinkle a little of the vanilla and lemon extracts over the layer and dot with ¼ of the butter cubes. Repeat layers until the potatoes, sugar mixture, extracts, and butter are used. Cover with foil and bake at 375 degrees for about 1½ hours until the potatoes are tender. Remove the foil, then bake an additional 30 minutes to caramelize the potatoes and syrup.

Candied Sweet Potatoes

Stewed Okra and Tomatoes

SERVES 4 OR 5

Okra is a vegetable you either love or hate. The main reason, I think, is because it gets slimy when you boil it. The acid in the tomatoes and even the onions cut the slime.

2 tablespoons vegetable oil or bacon grease
1 yellow onion, diced
1 pound fresh okra, sliced, or 1-pound bag frozen okra
14½-ounce can diced tomatoes with liquid
1 teaspoon salt
1 teaspoon pepper
¼ teaspoon crushed red pepper flakes

In a saucepan, add the oil or bacon grease and onions and cook for 3 to 5 minutes until soft. Add the okra, tomatoes, salt, pepper, and red pepper. Bring to a boil, then reduce heat to a simmer. Cook 15 to 20 minutes until the okra is tender.

Okra Fritters

SERVES 4 OR 5

Frying okra also eliminates the slime. We serve a lot of fried okra at the restaurant. These fritters are one way to eat fried okra. Try topping them with a little Quick Tomato Jam (recipe on page 82).

½ cup yellow or white cornmeal
¼ cup all-purpose flour
½ teaspoon salt
½ teaspoon pepper
¼ teaspoon dried thyme
pinch of cayenne pepper
½ cup diced onion
3 cups frozen okra slices, thawed and chopped
1 egg, beaten
½ cup buttermilk
oil

In a mixing bowl, combine the cornmeal, flour, salt, pepper, thyme, and cayenne. Add the onions and okra and coat well. In a separate small bowl, mix together the egg and buttermilk. Add to the okra mixture and mix until just combined. Heat about 1 inch of oil in a large skillet. Drop the batter into the hot oil by heaping tablespoons. Flatten slightly with the back of a spoon. Fry 2 to 3 minutes per side until golden

Okra Fritters

brown. Remove to drain on a sheet tray lined with paper towels. Serve hot. Makes about 20 fritters.

Quick Tomato Jam MAKES 2 CUPS

4 cups canned diced tomatoes
½ cup balsamic vinegar
1 cup sugar
1 teaspoon tarragon
2 teaspoons chopped garlic
¼ teaspoon crushed red pepper
   flakes
1 teaspoon thyme
1 teaspoon salt

Combine ingredients in a saucepan. Simmer for about 20 minutes until mixture reaches a jam-like consistency. Refrigerate before serving.

Corn Pudding

SERVES 8 TO 10

Can you actually go to a holiday meal or a potluck that doesn't include corn pudding?

2 tablespoons vegetable oil
1 onion, chopped
2 15¼-ounce cans sweet corn
2 14¾-ounce cans creamed corn
6 eggs, beaten
2 tablespoons cornmeal
2 tablespoons all-purpose flour
½ cup sugar
2 cups half-and-half
½ teaspoon salt
½ teaspoon white pepper
½ teaspoon dried thyme

Heat the oil in a skillet and cook onions until soft. In a large mixing bowl, add the onions along with remaining ingredients and mix well. Pour into a greased 4-quart casserole dish and bake at 350 degrees for 45 minutes to 1 hour, until a knife inserted in the middle comes out clean.

The source of our bounty

Summer's Bounty Succotash

SERVES 6 TO 8

2 cups fresh lima beans
½ teaspoon salt
2 or 3 strips bacon, chopped
4 or 5 ears corn, kernels removed
3 fresh tomatoes, peeled, seeded, and chopped
½ pound fresh okra, cut into ½-inch rounds
salt and pepper to taste

In a large saucepan, add the beans, salt, bacon, and enough water to cover by 2 inches. Bring to a boil, then simmer for 30 minutes until the beans are tender. Add the corn, tomatoes, and okra and continue to cook for an additional 20 minutes. Adjust salt and pepper.

Note To easily peel the tomatoes, make an *x* on the bottoms with a sharp paring knife and remove the cores. Drop the tomatoes in a pot of boiling water for 30 to 45 seconds. Remove to a pan of ice water. The skins will easily come off. Cut the tomatoes in half and squeeze to remove the seeds.

CHAPTER 4

STONE SOUL SIDES

Sides can be the lifesaver of the meal. If you're trying to stretch the main course of meat, you want people to fill up on sides. When you're having a large gathering, put the plates on the opposite end of the table from the meat. By the time your guests fill their plates with the sides, they'll have no space left for a lot of meat.

THE

LIFESAVER

OF THE

MEAL . . .

GERTRUDE'S MAC AND CHEESE

PIMENTO CHEESE MACARONI SOUFFLÉ

MACARONI SALAD

PASTA AND SEAFOOD SALAD

SIMPLE MASHED POTATOES

RICE AND GRAVY

DIRTY RICE

MS. ORA'S DOWN-HOME TATER SALAD

RED, WHITE, AND BACON POTATO SALAD

DEVILED EGGS

CRAB DEVILED EGGS

GREEN EGGS AND HAM

SMOKED SALMON DEVILED EGGS

BOURBON AND BACON BAKED BEANS

Gertrude's Mac and Cheese

SERVES 8 TO 10

Gertrude Joiner was Vivián's mother—the mother of six. A housewife with eight mouths to feed and a very small grocery "budget," she nonetheless fed her family well. Like my mom and many others, she figured out what to do with that big chunk of "government cheese."

16-ounce box elbow macaroni
1 pound extra-sharp cheddar cheese
½ pound Colby Jack cheese
1 stick butter, cubed
3 large eggs
½ cup milk

Cook the macaroni according to the package directions and drain. In a 4-quart casserole dish, add half of the macaroni, layer with half of both cheeses, and dot with half of the butter. Layer with the remaining macaroni, cheeses, and butter. In a small bowl, whisk together the eggs and milk. Pour mixture over the macaroni and cheese. Bake uncovered at 400 degrees for 20 to 25 minutes until the casserole is bubbly and golden brown.

Macaroni and Cheese and stuffing

Pimento Cheese Macaroni Soufflé

SERVES 4 OR 5

Everyone has a great macaroni and cheese recipe. This starts with a cheese sauce and cream cheese and includes the colorful addition of pimentos.

2 cups elbow macaroni
2 tablespoons butter
¼ cup flour
3 cups half-and-half
3 ounces cream cheese, cut into pieces
2 cups shredded yellow cheddar cheese, divided
4 eggs, beaten
½ teaspoon dry mustard
½ teaspoon paprika
1 teaspoon granulated garlic
pinch of cayenne pepper
2-ounce jar pimentos

Cook the macaroni according to the package directions. While the macaroni is cooking, add the butter and flour to a medium saucepan. Cook for 1 to 2 minutes and slowly whisk in the half-and-half. Heat to a simmer, then add the cream cheese and 1½ cups of the cheddar. Stir until the cheese has melted. Cook 3 to 4 minutes more. Add ¼ of the sauce into the eggs, then slowly whisk the eggs into the sauce. Stir in the mustard, paprika, garlic, and cayenne. Drain the macaroni and pour into a mixing bowl. Pour the cheese sauce onto the macaroni and stir to thoroughly coat. Add the pimentos and stir to combine. Pour into a greased 2-quart casserole dish and top with the remaining cheddar. Bake at 400 degrees for 20 to 25 minutes until the cheese is golden brown and bubbly.

Macaroni Salad

SERVES 8 TO 12

4 cups elbow macaroni
1 tablespoon salt
2 cups mayonnaise
2 teaspoons yellow mustard
2 teaspoons sugar
2 teaspoons apple cider vinegar
1 cup diced celery
1 yellow onion, diced
1 cup diced green pepper
½ cup pimentos
4 hard-cooked eggs
2 scallions, green parts only, chopped
salt and pepper to taste

Cook the macaroni with salt according to the package directions. Drain and rinse with cold water. In a small bowl, combine the mayonnaise, mustard, sugar, and vinegar. Place the macaroni in a large mixing bowl. Add the celery, onions, green peppers, and pimentos. Chop the eggs and fold into the macaroni, along with the scallions. Add the dressing and combine. Adjust salt and pepper. Refrigerate and serve cold.

Pasta and Seafood Salad

SERVES 4 TO 6

½ pound (2 cups) elbow macaroni
  or spiral pasta
1 pound medium cooked shrimp
10-ounce package imitation crabmeat
½ cup diced onion
½ cup diced green pepper
½ cup diced red pepper
½ cup diced celery
1 cup mayonnaise
6-ounce container plain Greek
  yogurt
½ cup mild chow-chow
2 teaspoons Old Bay seasoning
1 teaspoon dill
salt and pepper to taste

Cook the macaroni according to the package directions. Drain and rinse under cool water. Add the macaroni, shrimp, and crabmeat to a large bowl. Add the onions, green and red peppers, and celery. In a small bowl, mix together the mayonnaise, yogurt, chow-chow, Old Bay, and dill. Combine with the macaroni mixture. Adjust salt and pepper. Refrigerate at least 2 hours before serving.

Simple Mashed Potatoes

SERVES 4 OR 5

2 pounds russet potatoes
1 teaspoon salt
1 cup milk
2 tablespoons butter
salt and pepper to taste

Peel and quarter the potatoes. Add the potatoes to a medium pot, along with the salt and enough water to cover. Bring to a boil, then cook on medium heat for about 15 minutes until tender. Meanwhile, heat the milk to a simmer in a small saucepan. Drain the potatoes and transfer to a mixing bowl. Mash the potatoes with butter. Add the hot milk and stir until smooth. Add salt and pepper.

Rice and Gravy

Sometimes, this might be dinner. But more often, I'll have it alongside fried chicken. From the drippings of the chicken comes the gravy.

2 cups water
1 teaspoon salt
2 tablespoons butter
1 cup rice

Bring the water, salt, and butter to a boil in a medium saucepan. Stir in the rice and return to a boil. Boil for 2 to 3 minutes. Reduce the heat and cover the pan. Simmer over low heat for 20 to 25 minutes until all the liquid has been absorbed. Uncover and fluff the rice with a fork.

Gravy

4 tablespoons flour
4 tablespoons oil (remove all but 4 tablespoons of the oil from the skillet)
3 cups chicken broth or water
salt and pepper to taste

Add the flour and oil to a saucepan and cook until flour starts to brown. Slowly add the broth or water. Stir constantly with a fork or whisk until smooth and lump free. Cook for 6 to 7 minutes to remove the flour taste. Add salt and pepper and serve over rice.

Dirty Rice

I know there are a lot of dishes we should tweak for the sake of our arteries. I don't do it often enough, but I actually do it a little with Dirty Rice. You can use brown rice instead of white rice and turkey sausage instead of pork sausage.

½ pound country sausage
¼ pound chicken livers
2 teaspoons chili powder
½ teaspoon allspice
1 teaspoon dried thyme
¼ teaspoon cayenne pepper
1 cup chicken broth, divided
1 cup diced yellow onion
1 cup diced green pepper
1 cup diced celery
1 teaspoon chopped garlic
4 cups cooked rice
½ bunch scallions, green parts only, chopped
2 tablespoons chopped parsley

Cook the sausage and livers in a saucepan until they start to brown. With a wooden spoon, break up the livers and sausage. Add the chili powder, allspice, thyme, and cayenne. Add ¼ cup of the broth to the pan to get the browned bits, then add the onions, peppers, celery, and garlic. Cook until the vegetables are soft. Stir in the remaining stock and cooked rice. Stir to combine well and cook 5 to 8 minutes until the rice is heated through. Fold in the scallions and parsley.

Ms. Ora's Down-Home Tater Salad

SERVES 6 TO 8

Potato salad is always the barometer of an event. Like dry turkey, we talk about bad potato salad. The key is to salt the water you cook the potatoes in. And don't rinse the potatoes after they cook because it makes them soggy. Whenever we had an occasion for potato salad in our family, everyone looked to my grandmother to supply it. This is as close as I've come to re-creating her recipe.

3 pounds white potatoes, peeled and diced
2 tablespoons salt
½ cup diced celery
½ cup diced yellow onion
⅓ cup pickle relish
4 or 5 hard-cooked eggs, chopped
1 cup mayonnaise
1 tablespoon yellow mustard
2 or 3 shakes hot sauce
1 teaspoon granulated garlic
½ teaspoon onion powder
½ teaspoon salt
½ teaspoon pepper

Place the potatoes in a large pot with enough water to cover. Add the salt and bring potatoes to a boil, then simmer for about 10 minutes until they are just done. Drain the potatoes and cool slightly. Place them in a mixing bowl and add the celery, onions, relish, and eggs. In a separate bowl, combine the mayonnaise, mustard, hot sauce, garlic, onion powder, salt, and pepper. Mix well and add to the potatoes. Gently mix until well incorporated. Refrigerate for at least 2 hours or overnight before serving.

Red, White, and Bacon Potato Salad

SERVES 8 TO 12

2 pounds white potatoes, peeled
 and diced
1 tablespoon kosher salt
½ pound bacon, divided
3 pounds sweet potatoes, peeled
 and diced
2 cups diced celery
1 cup diced yellow onion
1 teaspoon granulated garlic
1½ teaspoons pepper
1½ teaspoons smoked paprika
1 tablespoon spicy brown mustard
¾ cup chow-chow or pickle relish
2 cups mayonnaise
5 hard-cooked eggs, chopped

Add the white potatoes, salt, and 1 strip of the bacon to a large pot. Add enough water to cover by 2 inches. Bring to a boil, then add the sweet potatoes. Simmer until the potatoes are still a little firm. Drain and allow to cool. The potatoes will continue to cook—be careful not to overcook them! Cook the remaining bacon until crisp. Drain and crumble. In a large mixing bowl, gently fold in all ingredients. Add more salt if necessary. Allow to sit refrigerated at least 2 hours or overnight before serving.

Deviled Eggs

MAKES 24

Is there ever an occasion that calls for food that doesn't include Deviled Eggs? They are a little time consuming but for the most part are worth it. There are many variations, and everyone has their own touch. But this covers the basics.

12 large eggs
¼ cup mayonnaise
1 tablespoon yellow mustard
1 tablespoon pickle relish
½ teaspoon salt
½ teaspoon white pepper
paprika for garnish

In a large saucepan, add the eggs and enough water to cover. (Adding about 1 tablespoon salt to the water will make peeling easier.) Bring to a boil. Lower the heat to a simmer and cook for 12 to 14 minutes. Remove from heat, drain, and run the eggs under cool water. Peel the eggs and cut in half. Scoop out the yolks into a bowl. Set the whites on a separate platter. Mash the yolks with a fork and add the mayonnaise, mustard, relish, salt, and white pepper. Mix well. Spoon a good amount of filling into the whites. Garnish with sprinkles of paprika.

Try some embellishments—please!

Deviled Eggs

Crab Deviled Eggs

MAKES 24

Prepare the Deviled Eggs above. Before filling the whites, add . . .

6-ounce can crabmeat, picked
1 tablespoon Worcestershire sauce
1 or 2 shakes Texas Pete
1 tablespoon Old Bay seasoning
chopped parsley for garnish

Fold the crabmeat into the yolk mixture. Add the Worcestershire, Texas Pete, and Old Bay. Scoop the filling into the egg whites and garnish with parsley.

Green Eggs and Ham

MAKES 24

12 large eggs, boiled and halved
1 ripe avocado
¼ cup mayonnaise
1 teaspoon lemon juice
½ cup chopped country ham
oil

Place the egg yolks in a medium bowl and mash them with a fork. Cut the avocado in half and remove the pit. Scoop out the meat of the avocado and add it to the yolks, along with the mayonnaise and lemon juice. Mix until smooth. In a sauté pan, cook the country ham with a little oil until crisp. Allow to cool. Spoon the yolk mixture into the egg whites and garnish with a little of the country ham.

Smoked Salmon Deviled Eggs

12 large eggs, boiled and halved
¼ cup mayonnaise
3-ounce package smoked salmon
  or lox
2 tablespoons sour cream
1 teaspoon chopped fresh dill
zest of 1 lemon
2-ounce jar red or black caviar
  (seriously, that stuff in the grocery store)

Scoop the yolks from the eggs into the bowl of a food processor. Reserve the whites to a platter. Add the mayonnaise and salmon or lox to the yolks and process until smooth. Remove to a small bowl and add the sour cream, dill, and lemon zest. Fill a pastry bag fitted with a star tip and pipe the yolk mixture into the egg whites, or spoon a generous amount into each egg. Top each egg with a dollop of caviar.

Bourbon and Bacon Baked Beans

Everybody has their favorite baked beans recipe (including the ones that come in the cans), but this has three of my favorite things: bourbon, bacon, and beans. It takes a little more time than most, but I think it's worth it.

1 pound thick bacon, diced 1 inch
1 onion, diced
1 pound navy beans, picked, rinsed, and soaked overnight
1 cup molasses
½ cup Dijon mustard
½ cup bourbon
salt and pepper to taste
1 teaspoon smoked paprika

Add the bacon to a Dutch oven and cook until it starts to brown. Add the onions and cook about 5 minutes until soft. Drain the beans and add to the pot with enough water to cover by 2 inches. Bring the pot to boil, then simmer for about 45 minutes until the beans are barely tender. Stir together the molasses, mustard, and bourbon and add to the pot. Cover, place in a 350-degree oven, and bake for 2 to 3 hours, occasionally checking and adding water as needed until the beans are tender. Remove the lid and season with salt and pepper and smoked paprika. Continue to cook an additional 30 to 45 minutes until the sauce thickens.

CHAPTER 5

HUMBLE BREAD, FEED MY SOUL

My family used to like bread. Growing up, we probably had some kind of bread at every meal. The kind of bread depended on what we were eating—cornbread with greens, biscuits with fried chicken, sometimes some kind of sweet bread at breakfast. Now, everybody seems to be afraid of bread. It's filled with gluten (heavy sigh).

Cornmeal and flour are staples. You know it's time to go to the grocery store when you're out of flour. Every culture seems to have its go-to breads—naan and chapati in India, baguettes in France, injera in Ethiopia and Eritrea, and biscuits in the South. We have cornbread, too, but biscuits are my favorite. Allow me to poeticize:

Ode to a Biscuit

A baguette, a croissant from Au Bon Pain,
 Injera or even some naan
Can't hold a stitch
To our Southern dish
Molasses with bis-cuit.
With country ham or strawberry jam,
 The taste is like no other.
With teary eye, a heavy sigh,
 Makes me long for my grandmother.

SOME KIND AT EVERY MEAL . . .

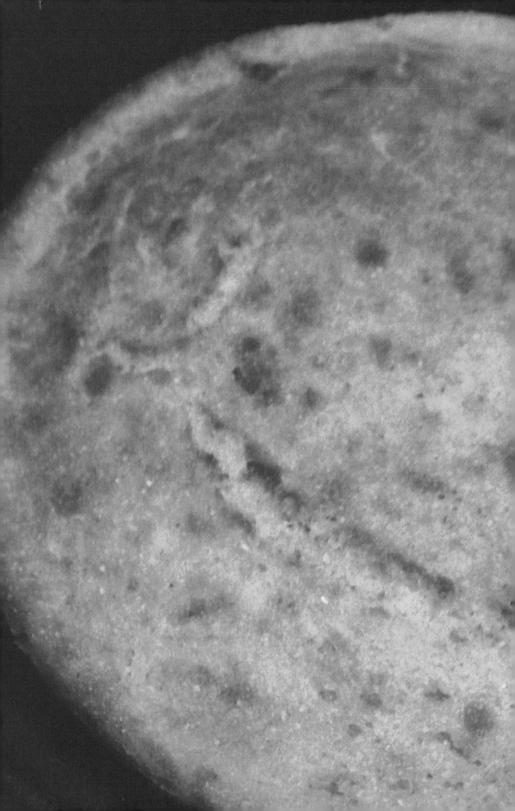

SKILLET CORNBREAD

CRACKLING CORNBREAD

HUSH PUPPIES

HOECAKES

BISCUIT HOECAKES

SPOON BREAD

TATER BREAD

BIG BUTTERMILK BISCUITS

CREAM BISCUITS

ANGEL BISCUITS

SIMPLE YEAST ROLLS

Skillet Cornbread

SERVES 8

Cornbread is one of those to-each-his/her-own things. Personally, I don't like sweet cornbread. My mom made Jiffy brand. It's very tender-sweet. Vivián likes *sweet* and is not a big fan of *crackling*. It's a matter of taste whether to use a mixture of flour and cornmeal or no flour at all. Feel free to adjust the amount of sugar, but I think the following is a good balance.

Regarding yellow cornmeal versus white, they're nearly interchangeable. It's like white grits and yellow grits. I prefer white cornmeal—grits as well. I believe there's a subtle difference in taste. Use what you have, but note that the look will vary—one will be whitish and the other yellow. I usually have white cornmeal on hand.

1½ cups white or yellow cornmeal
1 cup all-purpose flour
⅓ cup sugar
1 teaspoon baking powder
1 teaspoon baking soda
½ teaspoon salt
1 cup buttermilk
1 cup creamed corn
2 eggs
¼ cup vegetable oil

Place a greased cast-iron skillet in the oven while it preheats to 400 degrees. In a medium bowl, combine the cornmeal, flour, sugar, baking powder, baking soda, and salt. In a separate bowl, mix the buttermilk, creamed corn, eggs, and oil. Add the wet ingredients to the dry and mix to combine; do not overmix. Remove the skillet from the oven and pour the batter into it. Bake for 20 to 25 minutes until the cornbread is golden brown and the center is firm when touched.

Crackling Cornbread

SERVES 10

My favorite cornbread. Cracklings (the crispy leftovers from rendered pork fat) are readily available in most Southern groceries. I use white cornmeal, but yellow will work just as well.

2 tablespoons bacon grease
2½ cups white cornmeal
1 cup all-purpose flour
3 teaspoons baking powder
½ teaspoon baking soda
1 teaspoon salt
1 teaspoon sugar
2 cups cracklings
1 cup finely diced yellow onion
4 eggs, lightly beaten
2 cups buttermilk
2 tablespoons vegetable oil

Place the bacon grease in a 10-inch cast-iron skillet. Put the skillet in a 400-degree oven to heat while you make the batter. In a mixing bowl, combine the cornmeal, flour, baking powder, baking soda, salt, sugar, cracklings, and onions. Combine the eggs, buttermilk, and oil in a separate bowl. Add the egg mixture to the cornmeal and mix thoroughly. Remove the skillet from the oven and pour the batter into it. Return to the oven and bake for 20 to 25 minutes until the cornbread is golden brown and firm to the touch. The cornbread can also be baked in a traditional baking pan.

Hush Puppies

MAKES ABOUT 25

If you're not going to have a "light" bread at the fish fry, this is the thing.

2 cups white cornmeal
½ cup flour
1 teaspoon baking soda
2 teaspoons baking powder
1 teaspoon salt
¼ teaspoon sugar
¼ teaspoon cayenne pepper
¼ cup finely diced onion
1 egg, beaten
1¼ cups buttermilk
vegetable oil

In a medium mixing bowl, combine the cornmeal, flour, baking soda, baking powder, salt, sugar, cayenne, and onion. In a separate small bowl, mix together the egg and buttermilk. Add to the cornmeal mixture and mix well. Add 2 to 3 inches of oil to a Dutch oven or fryer and heat to 355 degrees. Carefully drop the batter into the oil by tablespoons. Fry until golden brown, turning with tongs. Remove from the oil to drain on a paper-towel-lined platter. Serve immediately.

Hoecakes

Hoecakes are a prime example of making the best with what you have. Slaves in the field used the blade of a hoe and flour or cornmeal—and ingenuity. When my mom wanted cornbread quickly to have with her buttermilk, this was her go-to. Quick, uncomplicated, and good.

1 cup self-rising cornmeal
¾ cup hot water
bacon drippings or vegetable oil

Add the cornmeal to a medium bowl. Slowly add the hot water and mix well. Heat the drippings or oil in a large skillet. Drop the batter by spoonfuls and spread into circles about 3 inches round. Fry 1 to 2 minutes on each side until brown.

Biscuit Hoecakes

SERVES 6 TO 8

My Mom's Aunt Sis liked these. Try them with molasses.

vegetable oil or bacon drippings
2 cups self-rising flour
½ cup shortening
1 cup milk

Place a cast-iron skillet containing about ¼ inch of oil or drippings into a 425-degree oven. In a medium bowl, add the flour and cut in the shortening using a fork or pastry cutter. Add the milk and stir to make a wet batter. Remove the skillet from the oven, pour the batter into it, and return it to the oven. Bake for 18 to 20 minutes until golden brown. A quicker method is to heat oil in a skillet or griddle, drop the batter in by spoonfuls, and fry it like pancakes, browning it on each side.

Serve immediately with a bowl of beans or molasses.

Spoon Bread

Spoon Bread is a cross between cornbread and corn pudding—a cornbread casserole. Simple and versatile.

1 cup cornmeal
4 cups milk
3 tablespoons melted butter
1 teaspoon salt
1 teaspoon sugar
4 eggs, separated

Preheat the oven to 375 degrees. Grease a 2-quart casserole dish and place it in the oven. Combine the cornmeal, milk, butter, salt, and sugar in a saucepan. Cook over moderate heat until the mixture is thick. Remove from heat and allow to cool slightly. Beat the egg yolks in a bowl and slowly add them to the cornmeal mixture. In a clean bowl, whip the egg whites to soft peaks. Fold the egg whites into the cornmeal. Remove the casserole dish from the oven and pour in the batter. Bake about 45 minutes until the Spoon Bread is set and golden.

Enhancements

Before removing the batter from the stove, stir in 1 cup of shredded cheddar cheese and/or 1 cup of crumbled, cooked country sausage.

Or add 1 cup of cooked, mashed sweet potatoes and a pinch of cinnamon.

Spoon Bread

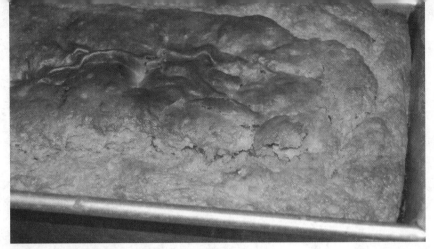

Tater Bread

MAKES 2 LOAVES

So many sweet potatoes, and so many things to do with them. Try this with strawberry preserves and country ham—yum!

5 cups all-purpose flour
¾ cup sugar
4½ teaspoons baking powder
1½ teaspoons baking soda
1 teaspoon salt
1 teaspoon cinnamon
¼ teaspoon ginger
¼ teaspoon nutmeg
2 cups cooked, mashed sweet potatoes
3 cups buttermilk
1 teaspoon vanilla extract
3 eggs, lightly beaten
¼ cup melted butter

Grease two 8-inch loaf pans. Preheat the oven to 350 degrees. In a large mixing bowl, combine the flour, sugar, baking powder, baking soda, salt, cinnamon, ginger, and nutmeg. In a separate bowl, stir together the sweet potatoes, buttermilk, vanilla, eggs, and butter. Add the buttermilk mixture to the flour mixture. Stir to combine, being careful not to overmix. Pour the batter into the prepared pans and bake for about 1 hour until a knife inserted into the center comes out clean. Allow to cool in the pans for 15 minutes before removing and slicing.

Tater Bread

Big Buttermilk Biscuits

MAKES ABOUT 12 BISCUITS

4 cups all-purpose flour
3 tablespoons baking powder
1 teaspoon salt
1 teaspoon sugar
¾ cup butter, chilled and cut into small cubes
1⅓ cups buttermilk, divided
¼ cup melted butter

In a large mixing bowl, combine the flour, baking powder, salt, and sugar. Cut in the butter using a pastry cutter or fork until the flour resembles coarse meal. Make a well in the flour and add 1 cup of the buttermilk. Using a rubber spatula or your hands, pull the flour into the milk. Don't overmix; mix just until all the flour has been incorporated. Add more buttermilk a little at a time to form a sticky dough. Turn the dough onto a lightly floured surface, pat it into a ½-inch-thick loaf, and fold in half. Repeat 2 more times until you have a smooth dough. Roll or pat the dough out to a ½-inch thickness and cut out biscuits using a 3-inch biscuit cutter. Spray a baking sheet with pan spray or line it with parchment paper. For soft-sided biscuits, place them on the sheet so they touch slightly. Bake at 425 degrees for 10 to 12 minutes until lightly browned. Remove from the oven and brush with melted butter.

For a variation, you can make Sweet Potato Biscuits by incorporating 1 cup of mashed or puréed sweet potatoes into the buttermilk and adding ½ teaspoon each of cinnamon and nutmeg to the flour mixture.

Cream Biscuits

MAKES 10 BISCUITS

It was the rarest of occasions when our household had biscuits that did not come from those cans you hit on the side of the table (which I loved to do). Some such occasions involved my grandmother. She would bring us biscuits she made; they were flat because my mother didn't like fluffy middles. My grandmother usually carried in her purse either fatback and a biscuit or a biscuit stuffed with country ham. Old habits die hard. Back in the day, when we traveled, it paid to be self-sufficient.

I'm sure my grandmother could make any type of bread or biscuit, but she favored these—very simple and quick.

2 cups self-rising flour
2 teaspoons sugar
1 cup heavy cream
butter

Preheat the oven to 450 degrees. Lightly spray a baking sheet with pan spray. Combine the flour and sugar in a medium mixing bowl. Form a well in the flour, add the cream, and stir until a stiff dough is formed; don't overmix. Turn the dough out on a lightly floured surface. With floured hands, form the dough into a ball, flatten slightly, and fold in half. Repeat this 2 or 3 times until the dough is not sticky. Pat out the dough about ½ inch thick. Cut biscuits using a floured 2-inch cutter. For soft-sided biscuits, place the biscuits on the baking sheet so they touch. For crispier-sided biscuits, place them on the sheet 1 inch apart. Bake for 10 to 12 minutes until lightly browned. Remove from the oven and brush with butter.

Angel Biscuits

These are biscuits with wings. They're light but sturdy enough for country ham—which is apparently my barometer for everything.

½-ounce packet yeast
¼ cup warm water
2 cups warm buttermilk
5 cups all-purpose flour
2 tablespoons sugar
1 tablespoon baking powder
1 teaspoon baking soda
1 teaspoon salt
1 cup chilled shortening
melted butter

In a small bowl, dissolve the yeast in warm water. Stir in the buttermilk. In a separate bowl, mix together the flour, sugar, baking powder, baking soda, and salt. Cut the shortening into the flour mixture with a pastry cutter or your fingertips until it resembles coarse meal. Stir the buttermilk mixture into the flour mixture and combine well. Turn the dough out onto a lightly floured surface. Fold the dough and knead it 4 or 5 times. Pat the dough out ½ inch thick. Cut out biscuits using a 2-inch cutter and place on a greased baking sheet 1 inch apart. Cover and let rise for 45 minutes until doubled in size. Bake at 450 degrees for 10 to 12 minutes until golden brown. Brush with melted butter.

Simple Yeast Rolls

MAKES 12 ROLLS

2 to 2½ cups all-purpose flour, divided
½-ounce packet yeast
2 tablespoons sugar
1 teaspoon salt
½ cup milk
¼ cup water
2 tablespoons butter
1 egg, beaten

Mix ¾ cup of the flour, yeast, sugar, and salt in a mixing bowl. Heat milk, water, and butter to 120 to 130 degrees. Add warm milk mixture and egg to the flour mixture and mix on low for 2 minutes. Gradually mix in the remaining flour to form a sticky dough. Turn the dough onto a floured surface and knead for 5 to 8 minutes until dough is smooth and springs back. Let the dough rest for 10 minutes. Divide it into 12 equal pieces and shape into balls. Place in a greased 9-inch round pan. Cover and let rise in a warm place for about 45 minutes until the dough has doubled in size. (If you turn your oven to low or warm, that's a good place to let the dough rise.) Heat the oven to 400 degrees and bake rolls for 12 to 15 minutes until golden brown. Brush with additional butter.

CHAPTER 6

THE SOUL-STIRRING POT

SOUPS AND STEWS

Soups and stews allow you to be gracious and say, "You better have some," when you don't have a lot. A pot of stew on the stove suggests comfort and home. My mother certainly was not the best cook in the world, but when she made her soup for us, from bits and pieces of previous meals, we were more than fed—we were loved.

YOU BETTER HAVE SOME . . .

EVERYTHING-IN-IT VEGETABLE SOUP (ICEBOX SOUP)

POTATO SOUP

CHICKEN SOUP

PINTO BEAN AND COUNTRY HAM SOUP

COLLARD GREENS STEW WITH CORNMEAL DUMPLINGS

CHICKEN AND SAGE DUMPLINGS

OXTAIL AND BUTTER BEAN STEW

BEEF STEW

CATFISH STEW

GOOD LUCK STEW

LUCKY VEGGIE STEW

Everything-in-It Vegetable Soup (Icebox Soup)

SERVES 8 TO 10

Truthfully, when we had this "vegetable" soup in our house, it more than likely had meat in it—leftover pot roast or beef stew, or some sort of pork that was in the freezer. It was definitely hearty. It and a piece of cornbread were sometimes the meal. And so I celebrate cleaning out the icebox.

2 tablespoons vegetable oil
2 cups diced carrots
1 cup diced celery
1 cup diced onion
1 tablespoon chopped garlic
2 teaspoons dried thyme
½ head cabbage, chopped
3 cups corn
2 cups any or all: green beans, cooked chicken, cooked beef, cooked pork, or whatever you have in the freezer
1 or 2 medium white and/or sweet potatoes, diced
14½-ounce can diced tomatoes
2 quarts beef or chicken broth
3-ounce can tomato paste
salt and pepper to taste

In a soup pot, heat the oil and sauté the carrots, celery, and onions for 3 to 5 minutes until soft. Add the garlic and thyme and sauté 1 minute more. Throw next 7 ingredients into the pot and simmer until the vegetables are tender and the soup has thickened. Adjust salt and pepper.

Potato Soup

SERVES 6 TO 8

Any cook will probably tell you that if you've got a potato and an onion in the house and your water hasn't been turned off, you've got a meal. My friend Arthur in Atlanta told me his grandmother would make him potato soup when he didn't feel well. It was so good that sometimes he would fake not feeling well just to get it. Comfort and joy!

¼ cup butter or oil
1 large yellow onion, diced
2 stalks celery, chopped
2 tablespoons all-purpose flour
6 cups water or chicken broth
3 pounds white potatoes, peeled
   and cut into 1½-inch pieces
1 cup milk
salt and pepper to taste

Place the butter or oil, onions, and celery in a soup pot and cook about 15 minutes until the vegetables are soft and the onions start to brown slightly. Stir in the flour. Add the water or broth and potatoes. Bring to a boil, then reduce to a simmer. Cook 15 to 20 minutes until the potatoes are soft. Add the milk and heat through. Adjust salt and pepper.

Enhancements

Stir some cheese and bacon or chopped ham into the hot soup. Garnish with chopped scallions.

Chicken Soup

SERVES 6 TO 8

This a great use for leftover chicken—including the carcass, if you use it for the stock. Add cooked rice or beans for a more substantial meal.

3 tablespoons oil
1 medium onion, chopped
2 teaspoons chopped garlic
2 medium carrots, peeled and
   diced
2 stalks celery, diced
1 tablespoon dried basil
2 teaspoons dried thyme
8 cups chicken broth
1 bay leaf
1½ cups egg noodles
1½ cups cooked chicken, shredded
1 cup canned diced tomatoes

Heat the oil in a soup pot and add the onions, garlic, carrots, and celery. Cook for 6 to 8 minutes until the vegetables are soft but not brown. Add the basil and thyme and cook 2 to 3 minutes more. Add the broth, bay leaf, and egg noodles and bring to a boil. Cook about 5 minutes until the noodles are soft. Fold in the chicken and tomatoes and heat through.

Pinto Bean and Country Ham Soup

SERVES 6 TO 8

1-pound bag pinto beans
2 smoked ham hocks
4 or 5 strips bacon
1 cup diced yellow onion
2 cups diced green pepper
1 cup chopped country ham
1 teaspoon chopped garlic
2 teaspoons dried thyme
2 teaspoons sage
¼ teaspoon crushed red pepper
  flakes
salt and pepper to taste
14½-ounce can diced tomatoes
1 bunch green onions, chopped

Sort through the beans to remove misshapen or discolored beans and stones. Soak the beans overnight.

Rinse the beans and add them to a large pot, along with the ham hocks and enough water to cover by 6 inches. Bring to a boil, then reduce heat to a simmer for 1 to 2 hours. Cook the bacon in a large sauté pan or skillet until crispy. Remove, crumble, and reserve the bacon. Add the onions, green peppers, country ham, garlic, thyme, sage, and red pepper to the pan and cook until the vegetables are soft. Add the vegetables and ham to the pot and cook for 1½ to 2 hours until the beans are soft. Adjust salt and pepper. Add the tomatoes and green onions and heat through. Stir in the crumbled bacon.

Collard Greens Stew with Cornmeal Dumplings

SERVES 6 TO 8

4 strips bacon
2 stalks celery, diced
1 green pepper, diced
1 large yellow onion, diced
4 quarts chicken stock or water
1 ham hock
3 pounds collard greens
¼ teaspoon crushed red pepper flakes
1 tablespoon dried thyme
1 tablespoon kosher salt
1 tablespoon pepper
14½-ounce can diced tomatoes

Add the bacon to a large Dutch oven or a pot with a tight-fitting lid and cook until crisp. Remove, crumble, and reserve. Add the celery, green peppers, and onions to the pot. Cook about 5 minutes until the vegetables are soft. Add the stock or water and ham hock. Bring to a boil, then simmer about 30 minutes until the meat is tender. Remove the ham hock from the pot, take the meat from the bone, and return the meat to the pot. Add the greens, red pepper, thyme, salt, and pepper. Simmer for 25 to 30 minutes. Add Cornmeal Dumplings (recipe below), cover the pot, and simmer 15 to 20 minutes more until the greens are tender and dumplings are puffed and cooked through. Stir in the diced tomatoes and reserved bacon.

Cornmeal Dumplings

½ cup flour
½ cup white or yellow cornmeal
1½ teaspoons baking powder
½ teaspoon salt
1 teaspoon sugar
2 tablespoons unsalted butter
½ cup buttermilk

Combine the flour, cornmeal, baking powder, salt, and sugar. Mix in the butter with a fork or your fingertips. Add the buttermilk. Stir until just combined. Form the dough into balls.

Chicken and Sage Dumplings

SERVES 6 TO 8

1 whole chicken, cut up
2 quarts chicken broth
1 or 2 stalks celery, chopped
1 onion, diced
2 carrots, peeled and diced
2 teaspoons dried thyme
1 bay leaf
1 clove garlic, smashed
10¾-ounce can cream of celery
  soup
chopped parsley for garnish

In a large soup pot, add the chicken, broth, celery, onions, carrots, thyme, bay leaf, and garlic. Bring to a boil. Reduce heat to a simmer and cook 15 to 20 minutes until the chicken is tender. Remove the chicken to a plate and allow to cool. Discard the skin and bones and return the chicken to the pot. Stir in the cream of celery soup and return the pot to a simmer. Drop Sage Dumplings (recipe below) by tablespoons into the pot. Keep the dumplings separate in the pot, as they will expand. Cover the pot and simmer 15 to 18 minutes until the dumplings are firm. Ladle into bowls and garnish with parsley.

Sage Dumplings

2 cups all-purpose flour
2 teaspoons baking powder
1 teaspoon salt
½ teaspoon pepper
1 teaspoon sage
2 eggs
2 tablespoons melted butter
¾ cup buttermilk

Combine the dry ingredients in a medium bowl. In a separate bowl, mix together the eggs, butter, and buttermilk. Add to the dry ingredients and combine to form a firm dough slightly thicker than pancake batter.

Oxtail and Butter Bean Stew

SERVES 4 TO 6

2½ cups dried butter beans
4 to 5 pounds oxtails
salt and pepper to taste
½ cup all-purpose flour
4 tablespoons vegetable oil
3 stalks celery, chopped
1 yellow onion, diced
2 large carrots, peeled and diced
1 tablespoon chopped garlic
1 tablespoon dried thyme
3 tablespoons tomato paste
2 14½-ounce cans diced tomatoes
with juice
4 cups beef broth
3 cups plain white rice, cooked

Soak the beans overnight.

Trim the excess fat from the oxtails and salt and pepper them liberally. In a medium bowl, add the flour and lightly coat oxtails. Heat the oil in a large Dutch oven or a heavy pot with a lid and brown the oxtails in batches. Remove to a platter. Add the celery, onions, and carrots. Cook 4 to 5 minutes until the vegetables begin to soften. Add the garlic and cook 1 minute more. Add the thyme, tomato paste, tomatoes, and broth. Return the oxtails to the pot, along with any accumulated juices. Bring the pot to a boil, then reduce heat. Cover and simmer for 2 hours. Drain and rinse the butter beans, then add them to the pot and continue to simmer an additional 2 to 2½ hours until the meat is very tender and the beans are done. Occasionally check the amount of liquid and adjust as needed. Serve hot over rice.

Baby
Lima   1.59 lb

Black eye
Pea

Beef Stew

¼ cup vegetable oil
½ cup flour, divided
1 teaspoon salt
½ teaspoon pepper
½ teaspoon granulated garlic
½ teaspoon dried thyme
2 pounds beef chuck or stew beef,
   cut into 1-inch pieces
1 large yellow onion, diced
2 tablespoons tomato paste
4 cups beef broth
2 cups peeled and diced carrots
2 cups peeled and diced white
   potatoes
2 stalks celery with leaves,
   chopped

Heat the oil in a Dutch oven or a pot with a lid. Combine ¼ cup of the flour, salt, pepper, garlic, and thyme in a bowl. Add the beef and toss to coat. Brown the beef in the oil in batches and remove to a platter. Place the onions in the pan and cook 6 to 8 minutes until soft. Stir in the tomato paste and remaining flour and cook another minute, then slowly stir in broth. Return the beef to the pot and bring to a boil. Cover and simmer for 2 hours. Remove the lid and add the carrots, potatoes, and celery. Cook until the meat is tender and vegetable are done. Season with salt and pepper.

Catfish Stew

SERVES 6 TO 8

My intention was to make fish-head stew. Vivián told me how her father made that stew for the family. She also told me, a little wistfully, how the kids in school made fun of her for eating said stew. So I gathered a few fish heads (butchers and fishmongers will provide anything if you're willing to pay) and proceeded to make the stew based on her description. I'll just say, "Eek!" Fish looking back at me with black eyeholes (you have to take the eyeballs out) was not very appealing. So I removed the fish heads and replaced them with fish. Catfish. But you can use any meaty fish you have on hand. The fish heads did make a nice, rich stock. The additional flavor was great.

3 or 4 strips bacon, chopped
1 cup diced yellow onion
1 cup diced green pepper
1 cup diced celery, leaves included
½ cup chopped carrots
1 teaspoon chopped garlic
1 tablespoon dried thyme
¼ cup tomato paste
2 bay leaves
4 fish heads, eyes removed (optional)
6 cups water or seafood stock
2 14½-ounce cans diced tomatoes with juice
2 cups peeled and diced white potatoes
1 cup peeled and diced sweet potatoes
1 to 2 pounds catfish fillets, cut into bite-sized pieces
1 tablespoon Worcestershire sauce
dash of Texas Pete
salt and pepper to taste

Add the bacon to a Dutch oven or a large pot with a lid. Cook until the fat has been rendered. Add the onions, green peppers, celery, and carrots. Sauté for 5 to 6 minutes until the vegetables are soft. Add the garlic and thyme and cook 1 minute more. Stir in the tomato paste. Add the bay leaves, fish heads (if using), water or stock, tomatoes, and potatoes. Bring to a boil, then cover and reduce heat to a simmer. Cook for about 15 minutes until the potatoes are tender. Remove the fish heads (if you like) and add the catfish. Cook for an additional 10 to 12 minutes until the fish is done. Stir in the Worcestershire and Texas Pete. Adjust salt and pepper.

Good Luck Stew

SERVES 8 TO 10

This one-pot stew has been our New Year's Day tradition at the restaurant for the past few years. It has never been our wish to leave anyone out of luck, so we also do a vegetarian version.

2 pounds neck bones
1 or 2 smoked ham hocks
3 cubes chicken or beef bouillon
1 yellow onion, chopped
2 or 3 whole cloves garlic
3 stalks celery with leaves, chopped
¼ teaspoon crushed red pepper flakes
1 tablespoon dried thyme
2 or 3 bay leaves
1 pound black-eyed peas
2 pounds collard greens, cleaned and chopped (or 1 bag pre-trimmed and washed greens)
1 tablespoon salt
white rice

In a large stockpot, add the neck bones, ham hocks, and enough water to cover. Bring to a boil and boil for 20 minutes. Remove the pot from the stove. Discard the water and rinse the meat; this helps get rid of the scum. Return the meat to the pot and add enough water to cover by 3 inches. Add bouillon, onions, garlic, celery, red pepper, thyme, and bay leaves. Bring to a boil, then lower heat to a simmer. Cover and cook for 1 hour. Rinse the black-eyed peas and add them to the pot. Continue to simmer for 30 minutes. Add the collards and salt. Cook about 1 more hour until the peas and greens are tender. Stir the pot to combine the greens and peas. Serve over white rice. If you are so inclined, remove the bones from the pot before serving.

Lucky Veggie Stew

SERVES 6 TO 8

No matter what you do or how hard you try to hide, you'll eventually host a food occasion that has someone who does not eat meat. A vegetarian. Just be forewarned, if you feed them this stew, especially with a piece of cornbread, they will *never* go away.

2 tablespoons olive oil
1 cup diced green pepper
1 cup diced onion
1 cup diced celery, leaves included
1 teaspoon chopped garlic
1 tablespoon curry powder
8 cups vegetable stock
2 cups black-eyed peas
1 pound collard greens, cleaned and chopped, tough stems removed
2 14½-ounce cans diced tomatoes
2 cups sliced fresh or frozen okra
1 large sweet potato, peeled and diced
salt and pepper to taste

Heat the oil in a Dutch oven or a large pot with a lid. Add the green peppers, onions, and celery. Cook 4 to 5 minutes until the vegetable begin to soften, then add the garlic and curry powder. Continue to cook for 1 minute until the curry becomes fragrant. Add the stock, black-eyed peas, greens, and tomatoes. Bring to a boil, then reduce heat, cover, and simmer for about 45 minutes until the beans are cooked. Remove the lid and add the okra and sweet potatoes. Continue cooking until the potatoes and vegetables are done. Season with salt and pepper.

CHAPTER 7

DESSERTS TO SELL YOUR SOUL FOR

It is said that man cannot live by bread alone. Sometimes, you need some *sugar*!

Picture the box lunch on that long trip up north—boiled eggs, cold fried chicken, a biscuit, and a piece of pound cake wrapped in wax paper. It's simple—dessert makes you feel better, even after a meager meal. Even if it means just chewing on a biscuit and molasses. Hug the cook who provides you with dessert.

SOMETIMES YOU
        NEED SOME SUGAR . . .

LEMON POUND CAKE

BANANA PUDDING

BUTTERMILK PIE

SWEET POTATO PIE

SWEET POTATO CAKE WITH BROWN SUGAR AND
BOURBON GLAZE

7UP CAKE

BUTTERMILK CAKE WITH CHOCOLATE FROSTING

PINEAPPLE-COCONUT CAKE

RICE PUDDING

BREAD PUDDING WITH BOURBON-CARAMEL
SAUCE

FRESH PEACH COBBLER WITH SWEET POTATO
BISCUIT CRUST

AUNT SIS`S GINGERBREAD

CORNMEAL CAKE

RED VELVET CAKE

BERNETHA WELDON`S RED VELVET POUND CAKE

Lemon Pound Cake

SERVES 8 TO 10

3 cups all-purpose flour
½ teaspoon baking powder
3 sticks butter
3 cups sugar
6 eggs
1 teaspoon vanilla extract
2 teaspoons lemon extract
1 cup milk

Sift the flour and baking powder into a bowl. Cream the butter and sugar in an electric mixer until light. Add the eggs 1 at a time, mixing well after each addition. Add the vanilla and lemon extracts to the milk. Add the dry ingredients to the butter alternately with the milk, beginning and ending with the flour. Pour batter into a greased and floured 10-inch tube pan. Place cake in a 350-degree oven for about 1 hour and 15 minutes, until a toothpick inserted into the center comes out clean.

Banana Pudding

SERVES 6 TO 8

I like my Banana Pudding topped with whipped cream. But there are those who can't eat it without meringue.

2 eggs plus 2 egg yolks
1 cup sugar
2 tablespoons flour
2 cups whole milk
1 tablespoon vanilla
2 tablespoons butter
1 pound bananas, sliced
11-ounce box vanilla wafers

Beat eggs and extra yolks well, then add sugar and flour. Pour in milk and simmer on top of a double boiler for 20 minutes, stirring constantly until the pudding starts to thicken. Remove from heat and add vanilla and butter. In a 9-inch pan or your favorite serving dish, layer bananas and vanilla wafers in 2 layers, ending with bananas. Pour pudding over bananas and wafers until pan is full. Top with vanilla wafers. Chill and serve topped with whipped cream or Meringue (recipe below).

Meringue

5 egg whites, room temperature
¼ teaspoon cream of tartar
2 tablespoons sugar
1 teaspoon vanilla extract

Using an electric mixer, beat the egg whites to soft peaks. Add the cream of tartar. Whip at high speed and sprinkle in the sugar 1 tablespoon at a time until stiff peaks form. Stir in the vanilla. Spread the Meringue over the pudding all the way to sides of pan. Bake in a 400-degree oven for 5 to 6 minutes until the Meringue browns.

Buttermilk Pie

MAKES 1 PIE

This is the basis of many chess pies. The commonality is making something delicious from simple ingredients on hand.

4 large eggs plus 2 egg yolks
1½ cups sugar
3 tablespoons melted butter
2½ tablespoons cornmeal
½ cup buttermilk, shaken well
½ teaspoon salt
1½ teaspoons vanilla extract
½ teaspoon nutmeg

Whisk together the eggs, egg yolks, and sugar until smooth. Add the remaining ingredients. Pour into a 9-inch unbaked pie shell and bake at 350 degrees for 40 to 45 minutes until the filling has puffed and browned slightly. The middle will be a little jiggly. Allow to cool before slicing.

Right: *Buttermilk Pie*

Sweet Potato Pie

What can I say? Should this be our national Thanksgiving Day dessert? My vote is yes!

For the most flavorful sweet potatoes for both Sweet Potato Pie and Sweet Potato Cake (page 147), bake the potatoes, then peel and purée them. In boiling, a lot of the flavor is lost in the water and the potatoes get water-logged.

2 cups baked, peeled, and puréed sweet potatoes
1 cup sugar
1 tablespoon flour
3 eggs, beaten
½ teaspoon cinnamon
½ teaspoon nutmeg
2 cups sweetened condensed milk
¼ cup melted butter
1 teaspoon vanilla extract
1 teaspoon lemon extract

Combine the sweet potatoes with sugar and flour. Stir in eggs and mix in cinnamon and nutmeg. Add remaining ingredients and mix until well combined. Pour into an unbaked 9-inch pie shell and bake at 350 degrees for about 45 minutes until done. Pie should rise slightly and middle should no longer look wet or shiny.

Sweet Potato Cake with Brown Sugar and Bourbon Glaze

SERVES 8 TO 10

4 eggs, beaten
2 cups sugar
1 cup olive oil
2 cups sifted flour
2 teaspoons baking soda
½ teaspoon salt
2 teaspoons cinnamon
½ teaspoon nutmeg
2 cups baked, peeled, and puréed
  sweet potatoes

In an electric mixer, combine the eggs, sugar, and olive oil. Mix together the flour, baking soda, salt, cinnamon, and nutmeg. Add the flour mixture to the eggs and mix well. Stir in the sweet potatoes and pour into a greased, floured Bundt pan. Bake at 350 degrees for 55 to 60 minutes until a toothpick inserted near the center comes out clean. Allow the cake to cool for 15 minutes, then invert onto a serving plate. Pour Brown Sugar and Bourbon Glaze (recipe below) over the cake.

Brown Sugar and Bourbon Glaze

1 cup light brown sugar
¼ cup butter
½ cup heavy cream
2 tablespoons bourbon
¾ cup powdered sugar

In a saucepan, combine the brown sugar, butter, cream, and bourbon. Bring to a boil, then reduce heat. Simmer for 3 to 4 minutes and remove from heat. Stir in the powdered sugar. Allow the glaze to cool.

7UP Cake

SERVES 10

1½ cups butter, softened
3 cups sugar
5 eggs
3 cups flour
2 teaspoons combination lemon
  extract and lemon zest
1 teaspoon vanilla extract
1 tablespoon lime zest or juice
¾ cup 7UP or other lemon-lime
  soda

Preheat the oven to 325 degrees. Grease and flour a 12-cup tube or Bundt pan. In a mixing bowl, cream the butter and sugar until light and fluffy. Add the eggs 1 at a time, beating well after each addition. Stir in the flour 1 cup at a time. Add the lemon extract and lemon zest, vanilla, and lime zest or juice. Pour the 7UP into the batter. Pour the batter into the prepared pan and bake for about 1 hour until a toothpick inserted in the center comes out clean. Allow the cake to cool in the pan for 15 minutes, then invert onto a serving plate. Decorate with Glaze (recipe below).

Glaze

2 cups powdered sugar
1 tablespoon fresh lemon juice
2 to 3 tablespoons Key lime juice

In a small bowl, mix together the sugar and juices. Pour over the cooled cake.

Buttermilk Cake with Chocolate Frosting

SERVES 8

1 cup softened butter
2 cups sugar
4 eggs plus 2 egg yolks
1 teaspoon salt
3 teaspoons baking powder
3 cups flour
2½ teaspoons vanilla extract
1 teaspoon almond extract
2 cups buttermilk

Cream the butter and sugar with an electric mixer until light and fluffy. Add the eggs and extra yolks 1 at a time. In a separate bowl, combine the salt, baking powder, and flour. Mix the vanilla and almond extracts with the buttermilk. Add flour mixture and buttermilk mixture alternately to the egg mixture, beginning and ending with the flour. Pour batter into 2 greased and floured 9-inch pans. Bake at 350 degrees for about 20 minutes until a toothpick inserted in the center comes out clean. Allow cakes to cool in pans for 10 minutes. Remove cakes from pans and allow them to cool completely on a wire rack before icing with Chocolate Frosting (recipe below).

Chocolate Frosting

2¾ cups chocolate chips
1 cup butter
4 cups powdered sugar
½ cup milk or half-and-half

In a saucepan, combine the chocolate chips and butter. Cook over low heat until chocolate has melted. Allow to cool. Add the chocolate and powdered sugar to a mixing bowl. Mix until smooth. Add the milk or half-and-half until mixture reaches a spreading consistency.

Pineapple-Coconut Cake

SERVES 8

Buttermilk Cake is very versatile. With the addition of coconut flavoring, it becomes a whole other cake.

1 cup softened butter
2 cups sugar
4 eggs plus 2 egg yolks
1 teaspoon salt
3 teaspoons baking powder
3 cups flour
1 teaspoon vanilla extract
2 teaspoons coconut extract
2 cups buttermilk

Cream the butter and sugar with an electric mixer until light and fluffy. Add the eggs and extra yolks 1 at a time. In a separate bowl, combine the salt, baking powder, and flour. Mix the vanilla and coconut extracts with the buttermilk. Add flour mixture and buttermilk mixture alternately to the egg mixture, beginning and ending with the flour. Pour batter into 2 greased and floured 9-inch pans. Bake at 350 degrees for about 20 minutes until a toothpick inserted in the center comes out clean. Allow cakes to cool in pans for 10 minutes. Remove cakes from pans and allow to cool completely on a wire rack before icing.

Pineapple Filling

20-ounce can crushed pineapple
½ cup sugar
2 tablespoons cornstarch
1 teaspoon lemon extract

Place the pineapple, sugar, and cornstarch in a saucepan. Bring to a boil, then reduce to a simmer. Cook 3 to 4 minutes until the sauce thickens. Remove from heat and add the lemon extract. Allow to cool.

Frosting

1½ cups light corn syrup
4 egg whites
3 sticks unsalted butter
½ teaspoon coconut extract
2 cups sweetened coconut, divided

In a small saucepan, heat the corn syrup to a boil. In the bowl of an electric mixer, whip the egg whites to soft peaks. Pour the corn syrup in a steady stream into egg whites with the mixer set to high. Add the butter 1 tablespoon at a time until mixture is smooth. Stir in the coconut extract and half of the coconut.

To assemble, spread the Pineapple Filling between the cake layers. Cover the cake with Frosting and sprinkle remaining coconut on sides and top of cake.

Rice Pudding

SERVES 5 OR 6

This is a great way to utilize leftover rice.

2 cups cooked rice
¼ cups raisins (optional)
3 eggs
1½ cups sugar
2 cups milk
1 teaspoon vanilla extract
½ teaspoon lemon extract
¼ teaspoon nutmeg
¼ teaspoon cinnamon

Butter a 1-quart casserole dish. Add the rice and raisins (if using). Beat the remaining ingredients in a small mixing bowl and pour over rice. Bake uncovered at 350 degrees for 30 to 40 minutes until a knife inserted into the center comes out dry. Serve warm or cold.

Bread Pudding with Bourbon-Caramel Sauce

SERVES 5 OR 6

This is another way to utilize leftovers. I've used leftover biscuits to make this Bread Pudding. It makes for a denser pudding. But any soft bread will work.

6 cups day-old bread
½ cup raisins (optional)
3 cups milk
4 eggs, beaten
2 cups sugar
1 tablespoon vanilla extract
2 teaspoons almond extract
¼ cup melted butter

Butter a 9-by-13-inch casserole dish. Layer the bread and raisins (if using) in dish. In a mixing bowl, combine the milk, eggs, sugar, vanilla and almond extracts, and butter. Pour over the bread and raisins. Stir the mixture to coat the bread. Allow to sit for about 10 minutes. Bake at 350 degrees for 40 to 50 minutes until the pudding is set and starts to brown on the edges. Serve warm with Bourbon-Caramel Sauce (recipe below).

Bourbon-Caramel Sauce

1 cup sugar
¼ cup water
½ teaspoon lemon juice
2 tablespoons bourbon
2 cups heavy cream

In a heavy saucepan, add the sugar, water, and lemon juice. Cook over medium heat for about 15 minutes until the sugar turns a caramel color. Carefully add the bourbon, cook 1 minute more, and remove from heat. Slowly whisk in the cream. The sauce will bubble a little. Continue to stir until smooth. Refrigerate the sauce. It will thicken as it cools.

Fresh Peach Cobbler with Sweet Potato Biscuit Crust

10 to 12 fresh peaches
1 tablespoon lemon juice
1 cup sugar (more or less depending on how sweet peaches are)
3 tablespoons cornstarch
1 teaspoon cinnamon
1 teaspoon almond extract
2 tablespoons butter

Bring a large pot of water to a boil. Make a small *x* on the bottom of each peach. Drop the peaches into boiling water for 45 to 60 seconds, then remove them to an ice bath. The peaches should peel easily. Peel them starting from the *x* on the bottom, then pit and slice them. Toss the peaches in a large bowl with the lemon juice, sugar, cornstarch, cinnamon, and almond extract. Arrange in a layer in a 9-by-13-inch baking dish. Dot with the butter. Cover with foil and bake in a 350-degree oven for 15 to 20 minutes. Remove the peaches from the oven. Remove the foil. Drop Sweet Potato Biscuit Crust dough (recipe below) by spoonfuls over the hot filling. Return to the oven and bake for 20 to 25 minutes until crust is browned and cooked through and fruit is bubbling. Cool slightly before serving.

Sweet Potato Biscuit Crust

1 cup all-purpose flour
¼ cup sugar
1¾ teaspoons baking powder
¼ teaspoon salt
pinch of cinnamon
¼ cup chilled butter
¼ cup milk
1 baked sweet potato, cut in half, peeled, and mashed
1 teaspoon vanilla

In a medium bowl, stir together the flour, sugar, baking powder, salt, and cinnamon. Using your fingers or a pastry cutter, cut the butter into the flour mixture until it resembles coarse meal. In a small bowl, combine the milk, sweet potato, and vanilla. Stir into the dry mixture, mixing well.

Aunt Sis's Gingerbread

SERVES 8 TO 10

Annie McCracken was my grandmother's older sister. We called her "Aunt Sis." She was the cake baker of the family and the oldest of the six sisters. They all had their specialties. My grandmother made great pies and fried chicken. Aunt Sis made the *best* Gingerbread.

2 cups all-purpose flour
½ cup sugar
2 teaspoons cinnamon
1 tablespoon dried ginger
½ teaspoon baking soda
¼ teaspoon salt
1 cup molasses
½ cup butter, cut into small cubes
¾ cup boiling water
1 egg, lightly beaten

Preheat the oven to 350 degrees. Lightly grease and flour a 9-inch cake pan. In a medium mixing bowl, combine the flour, sugar, cinnamon, ginger, baking soda, and salt. In a separate bowl, combine the molasses, butter, and boiling water and stir until butter is melted. Add the molasses mixture to the flour mixture, along with the beaten egg. Mix on medium speed for 2 minutes. Pour into the prepared pan. Bake 30 to 40 minutes until a toothpick inserted in the center comes out clean. Serve warm plain or with Lemon Curd (recipe below).

Lemon Curd

1 cup lemon juice
1 cup sugar
½ cup melted butter
4 eggs

Mix the ingredients well and place in a large microwave-safe bowl. Microwave on high in 1-minute increments, stirring after each. The total cooking time will be 7 to 10 minutes, depending on the microwave. The curd is done when it's thick enough to coat the back of a spoon. Refrigerate at least 2 hours before serving.

Aunt Sis's Gingerbread

Cornmeal Cake

SERVES 8 TO 10

Aunt Sis also made this Cornmeal Cake. She had a lot of mouths to feed (her only daughter had ten children!), so I got to taste only a small piece. I've been searching for that flavor ever since. It was cornbread but sweeter and eggier, with a hint of lemon. I love that ability to create something so memorable and delicious from something so simple.

1⅓ cups all-purpose flour
1 cup yellow cornmeal
1½ cups sugar
2 teaspoons baking soda
¼ teaspoon salt
3 eggs, lightly beaten
1½ cups buttermilk
¾ cup melted butter
1 teaspoon vanilla extract
½ teaspoon lemon extract

Combine the flour, cornmeal, sugar, baking soda, and salt in a medium mixing bowl. In a separate bowl, whisk together the eggs, buttermilk, butter, and vanilla and lemon extracts. Fold egg mixture into flour mixture and mix until well blended. Pour into a buttered 10-inch cast-iron skillet and bake at 375 degrees until the cake is golden brown and a toothpick inserted near the middle comes out dry. Allow to cool slightly and serve directly from the skillet.

Red Velvet Cake

Red Velvet Cake

SERVES 10 TO 12

2½ cups all-purpose flour
1½ cups sugar
1 teaspoon baking soda
1 teaspoon salt
2 tablespoons cocoa powder
1½ cups vegetable oil
1 cup buttermilk
2 eggs
2 tablespoons red food coloring
1 teaspoon white distilled vinegar
1 teaspoon vanilla extract
1 teaspoon almond extract

Preheat oven at 350 degrees. Grease and flour three 9-inch cake pans. In the bowl of an electric mixer, combine the flour, sugar, baking soda, salt, and cocoa powder. In a separate bowl, combine the vegetable oil, buttermilk, eggs, food coloring, vinegar, and vanilla and almond extracts. Mix well. Add the wet ingredients to the dry ingredients in thirds, mixing well with each addition. Divide the batter into prepared pans. Bake 25 to 30 minutes until a toothpick inserted in the center comes out clean. Remove cakes from pans and allow to cool before icing.

Frosting

2 8-ounce packages cream cheese, softened
½ cup softened butter
2 1-pound boxes powdered sugar
2 teaspoons vanilla extract
1 to 2 tablespoons milk or half-and-half

Beat the cream cheese and butter with an electric mixer on medium speed. Add the powdered sugar and blend until smooth. Add the vanilla. Thin the frosting with milk or half-and-half as needed to achieve a spreading consistency.

Bernetha Weldon's Red Velvet Pound Cake

SERVES 10 TO 12

Bernetha Weldon was the grandmother of one of our cooks at Sweet Potatoes, Tarhesia McKnight. Cooking can be learned, but caring cannot. Feeding a large family (thirteen people in a three-bedroom house) the basics is one thing. But adding dessert is the soul in soul food.

3 cups sugar
½ cup vegetable shortening
2 sticks butter
5 large eggs
¼ cup cocoa powder
1 teaspoon vanilla extract
pinch of salt
2 tablespoons red food coloring
3 cups all-purpose flour
¼ teaspoon baking powder
1 cup milk

Cream the sugar, shortening, and butter with an electric mixer until light and fluffy. Add the eggs 1 at a time, mixing just until blended after each addition. Stir in the cocoa powder, vanilla, salt, and food coloring. In a separate bowl, combine the flour and baking powder. Add the flour mixture to the egg mixture alternately with the milk, beginning and ending with the flour. Pour the batter into a greased and floured 10-inch tube pan. Bake

Red Velvet Pound Cake

at 300 degrees for about 1½ hours
until a toothpick inserted in the center
comes out clean. Remove the cake from
the pan to a wire rack. Drizzle Cream
Cheese Glaze (recipe on page 162) over
warm cake. Allow the cake to cool completely before slicing.

Cream Cheese Glaze

2 3-ounce packages cream cheese, softened
½ cup powdered sugar
1 teaspoon vanilla extract
2 or 3 tablespoons milk
finely chopped pecans or walnuts (optional)

Beat the cream cheese until smooth. Add the powdered sugar. Stir in the vanilla and milk until the mixture is of the consistency to drizzle over the cake. Garnish with pecans or walnuts if desired.

CHAPTER 8

SOULFUL CELEBRATIONS

MENUS TO PONDER

Food is the centerpiece of so much in our lives, especially in the South. We put forward our very best for the holidays. Growing up, we never had fewer than six side dishes and four desserts at Thanksgiving. As an adult, I've been trying to pare down the amount I cook during the holidays, to no avail. Old habits die hard. Not habits, I suppose, but tradition. Food is kindness. We offer it as a way to feed not just the body but also the soul during both celebrations and times of loss. Food and its preparation can release a kind of joy. It's the best thank-you when someone asks, "Who made the potato salad?" and are disappointed when they find out it's not *yours*.

These menus are merely a reflection of my soul food odyssey, which I hope will continue to evolve and become food for all souls.

FOOD IS KINDNESS . . .

CELEBRATE!

THANKSGIVING

SHERRY HANNAH'S ABSOLUTELY FABULOUS HAM

HOLIDAY ROAST TURKEY WITH CORNBREAD STUFFING AND
FRESH CRANBERRY AND ORANGE SAUCE

GIBLET GRAVY

SIMPLE MASHED POTATOES

GERTRUDE'S MAC AND CHEESE

QUICK(ER) POT OF GREENS

SWEET POTATO PIE

SWEET POTATO CAKE WITH BROWN SUGAR AND BOURBON
GLAZE

CHRISTMAS

STEPHANIE'S SLOW COOKER POT ROAST

FRIED CHICKEN

MS. ORA'S DOWN-HOME TATER SALAD

GREEN BEANS COOKED IN THE WAY OF THE SOUTH WITH
WHITE POTATOES

FRIED CABBAGE

BIG BUTTERMILK BISCUITS OR SKILLET CORNBREAD

BERNETHA WELDON'S RED VELVET POUND CAKE

BANANA PUDDING

NEW YEAR'S DAY

GOOD LUCK STEW OR LUCKY VEGGIE STEW

FRIED HOG JOWLS

SKILLET CORNBREAD

AUNT SIS'S GINGERBREAD

LEMON POUND CAKE

EASTER

VARIETY OF DEVILED EGGS

COUNTRY HAM WITH MOLASSES-DIJON MUSTARD GLAZE

FRIED TURKEY

SPICY COLLARD GREENS

GERTRUDE'S MAC AND CHEESE

CANDIED SWEET POTATOES

CREAM BISCUITS AND CRACKLING CORNBREAD

PINEAPPLE-COCONUT CAKE

BUTTERMILK PIE

FAMILY REUNIONS

LOW COUNTRY BOIL

SLAP YO' MAMMA! BBQ SPARE RIBS

RED, WHITE, AND BACON POTATO SALAD

PASTA AND SEAFOOD SALAD

FRESH PEACH COBBLER WITH SWEET POTATO BISCUIT

BID WHIST PARTIES

BRING YOUR OWN ADULT BEVERAGE

COUNTRY HAM

CREAM BISCUITS

MACARONI SALAD

7UP CAKE

FUNERAL REPASTS

FRIED CHICKEN

SMOTHERED PORK CHOPS

RICE AND GRAVY

GREEN BEANS COOKED IN THE WAY OF THE SOUTH WITH
WHITE POTATOES

SIMPLE YEAST ROLLS

LEMON POUND CAKE

BUTTERMILK CAKE WITH CHOCOLATE FROSTING

INDEX

Beans

Bourbon and Bacon Baked Beans, 102Good Luck Stew, 137

Green Beans Cooked in the Way of the South with White Potatoes, 77
Oxtail and Butter Bean Stew, 131
Pinto Bean and Country Ham Soup, 128
Summer's Bounty Succotash, 84

Beef

Beef Short Ribs, 56
Beef Stew, 134
Beef-A-Roni, 56-57
Liver and Onions, 57
Stephanie's Slow Cooker Pot Roast, 55

Breads

Angel Biscuits, 119
Big Buttermilk Biscuits, 116
Biscuit Hoecakes, 111
Cornbread, 48
Crackling Cornbread, 108
Cream Biscuits, 118
Hoecakes, 110
Hush Puppies, 109
Simple Yeast Rolls, 120
Skillet Cornbread, 107
Spoon Bread, 112
Tater Bread, 113

Cabbage

Braised Country Ribs with Smoked Sausage and Sauerkraut, 30
Creamy Coleslaw, 60

Fried Cabbage, 76
Sauerkraut, 30
Smothered Cabbage and Collard Greens, 75

Chicken

Ain't No Thing Like Spicy Chicken Wings, 41
Chicken and Sage Dumplings, 130
Chicken Soup, 127
Company's Coming Roast Chicken and Vegetables, 42-43
Dirty Rice, 94
Everyday BBQ Chicken, 43
Fried Chicken Livers, 44-45
Fried Chicken, 39
Oven-"Fried" Buttermilk Chicken, 40
Smothered Chicken Livers, 45
Stewed Chicken and Rice, 44

Corn

Corn Pudding, 83
Cornbread Stuffing, 48
Cornbread, 48
Crackling Cornbread, 108
Low Country Boil, 62-63
Skillet Cornbread, 107
Summer's Bounty Succotash, 84

Desserts

7UP Cake, 148
Aunt Sis's Gingerbread, 154
Banana Pudding, 143
Bernetha Weldon's Red Velvet Pound Cake, 160-62
Bread Pudding with Bourbon-Caramel Sauce, 152

Buttermilk Cake with Chocolate Frosting, 149

Buttermilk Pie, 144

Cornmeal Cake, 158

Fresh Peach Cobbler with Sweet Potato Biscuit Crust, 153

Lemon Curd, 154

Lemon Pound Cake, 143

Meringue, 144

Pineapple-Coconut Cake, 150-51

Red Velvet Cake, 159–60

Rice Pudding, 161

Sweet Potato Cake with Brown Sugar and Bourbon Glaze, 147

Sweet Potato Pie, 146

Eggs

Crab Deviled Eggs, 100

Deviled Eggs, 99

Fried Rice, Salmon, and Eggs, 66

Green Eggs and Ham, 100

Ms. Ora's Down-Home Tater Salad, 95

Pimento Cheese Macaroni Soufflé, 90

Red, White, and Bacon Potato Salad, 98

Smoked Salmon Deviled Eggs, 101

Fish & Seafood

Big Fried Real Shrimp, 64

Carolina Crab Cakes, 58

Catfish Stew, 135

Crab Deviled Eggs, 100

Fish Fry, 59-60

Fried Rice, Salmon, and Eggs, 66

Good Luck Stew, 137

Low Country Boil, 62-63

Pasta and Seafood Salad, 92

Salmon Croquettes, 65

Smoked Salmon Deviled Eggs, 101

Greens (Collard, Mustard, Turnip, Kale)

Collard Greens Stew with Cornmeal Dumplings, 129

Fried Chitterlings and Mustard Green Salad, 16

Good Luck Stew, 137

Lucky Veggie Stew, 138

Quick(er) Pot of Greens, 74

Smothered Cabbage and Collard Greens, 75

Spicy Collard Greens, 71

Ham

Country Ham with Molasses–Dijon Mustard Glaze, 24-26

Country Ham with Red-Eye Gravy over Creamy Grits, 27

Green Eggs and Ham, 100

Pinto Bean and Country Ham Soup, 128

Sherry Hannah's Absolutely Fabulous Ham, 23-24

Icings & Dessert Toppings

Brown Sugar and Bourbon Glaze, 147

7UP Cake Glaze, 148

Chocolate Frosting, 149

Pineapple Filling, 150

Pineapple-Coconut Cake Frosting, 151

Bourbon-Caramel Sauce, 152

Red Velvet Cake Frosting, 160

Red Velvet Pound Cake Cream Cheese Glaze, 162

Okra

Lucky Veggie Stew, 138

Okra Fritters, 81-82
Stewed Okra and Tomatoes, 81
Summer's Bounty Succotash, 84

Pasta, Dumplings, & Grits
Beef-A-Roni, 56-57
Chicken and Sage Dumplings, 130
C-Loaf and Spaghetti with Collard Green Pesto, 17-18
Collard Greens Stew with Cornmeal Dumplings, 129
Creamy Grits, 27
Gertrude's Mac and Cheese, 89
Macaroni Salad, 91
Pasta and Seafood Salad, 92
Pimento Cheese Macaroni Soufflé, 90
Sage Dumplings, 130

Peas
Black-Eyed Peas, 78
Good Luck Stew, 137
Lucky Veggie Stew, 138

Pork
Braised Country Ribs with Smoked Sausage and Sauerkraut, 30
C-Loaf and Spaghetti with Collard Green Pesto, 17-18
Country Ham with Molasses–Dijon Mustard Glaze, 24-26
Country Ham with Red-Eye Gravy over Creamy Grits, 27
Fatback, 32
Fried Chitterlings and Mustard Green Salad, 16
Fried Chitterlings, 14
Fried Hog Jowls, 34

Fried Pork Chop Sandwich, 22-23
Good Luck Stew, 137
Green Eggs and Ham, 100
Grilled BBQ'd Pigs' Feet, 19-20
Mr. Willie's Chitterlings, 13-14
Neck Bones and Pig Tails, 21
Pigs' Feet, 19
Sherry Hannah's Absolutely Fabulous Ham, 23-24
Slap Yo' Mamma! BBQ Spare Ribs, 28-29
Slow Cooker Boston Butt (Pork Shoulder), 31
Smothered Pork Chops, 22

Potatoes
Baked Sweet Potatoes, 79
Candied Sweet Potatoes, 80
Company's Coming Roast Chicken and Vegetables, 42-43
Green Beans Cooked in the Way of the South with White Potatoes, 77
Lucky Veggie Stew, 138
Ms. Ora's Down-Home Tater Salad, 95
Potato Soup, 126
Red, White, and Bacon Potato Salad, 98
Simple Mashed Potatoes, 92
Sweet Potato Pie, 146
Tater Bread, 113

Rice
Dirty Rice, 94
Fried Rice, Salmon, and Eggs, 66
Rice and Gravy, 93
Rice Pudding, 161
Rice, 44
Stewed Chicken and Rice, 44

Sausage & Bacon

Braised Country Ribs with Smoked Sausage and Sauerkraut, 30
Dirty Rice, 94
Low Country Boil, 62-63
Red, White, and Bacon Potato Salad, 98
Rice and Gravy, 93
Smoked Sausage, 30

Sauces, Rubs, Dressings, Gravy

Apple Cider Vinaigrette, 16
Collard Green Pesto, 18
Easy Cocktail Sauce, 63
Fresh Cranberry and Orange Sauce, 49
Giblet Gravy, 47
Have Mercy! Glaze, 41
Herbed Tartar Sauce, 59
Molasses–Dijon Mustard Glaze, 24
Neck Bones and Pig Tail Gravy, 21
Quick Tomato Jam 82
Red-Eye Gravy, 27
Rib Rub, 28
Rice and Gravy, 93
Seriously Good BBQ Sauce, 29
Sherry Hannah's Ham Glaze, 24

Soups and Stews

Beef Stew, 134
Catfish Stew, 135
Chicken and Sage Dumplings, 130
Chicken Soup, 127
Collard Greens Stew with Cornmeal Dumplings, 129
Everything-in-It Vegetable Soup (Icebox Soup), 125
Good Luck Stew, 137
Homemade Turkey Stock, 53
Lucky Veggie Stew, 138
Oxtail and Butter Bean Stew, 131
Pinto Bean and Country Ham Soup, 128
Potato Soup, 126

Tomatoes

Lucky Veggie Stew, 138
Stewed Okra and Tomatoes, 81
Summer's Bounty Succotash, 84

Turkey

Fried Turkey, 50-52
Holiday Roast Turkey with Cornbread Stuffing and Fresh Cranberry and Orange Sauce, 46-49
Smothered Turkey Wings x 2, 54
Turkey Hash, 52-53

Vegetables

Baked Sweet Potatoes, 79
Black-Eyed Peas, 78
Candied Sweet Potatoes, 80
Corn Pudding, 83
Fried Cabbage, 76
Green Beans Cooked in the Way of the South with White Potatoes, 77
Okra Fritters, 81
Quick(er) Pot of Greens, 74
Smothered Cabbage and Collard Greens, 75
Spicy Collard Greens, 71
Stewed Okra and Tomatoes, 82
Summer's Bounty Succotash, 84